UNMASKING THE INTERNET FOR RESEARCH

USING HANDS-ON ACTIVE LEARNING EXERCISES

Active Learning Series No. 2

Marilyn P. Whitmore
Contributing Editor

Contributors:

John J. Burke
Ruth J. Byers
Elizabeth W. Carter
Emaly Conerly
Barbara L. Cressman
Ann P. Daily
Katherine C. Ehrlich
Elaine Gass
Bruce Harley
Judith K. Hart
Janet McNeil Hurlbert
Marcia King-Blandford

Thura R. Mack
Pixie Anne Mosley
Necia Parker-Gibson
Ann Perbohner
Linda Ross
Sharon K. Sandall
Gail M. Staines
Ru Story-Huffman
Irene Weiner
Marilyn P. Whitmore
Daniel Yi Ziao

Library Instruction Publications

Library of Congress Catalog Card Number: 97-072733
ISBN:0-9652711-1-0

Printed by Whitmore Printing & Typesetting in Lancaster, Pennsylvania

Contents

Topic Oriented Internet Navigation

Preface

Does the Internet supply tools for education?

Here is what one student says:

> "As the Internet expands to include more and more sources of information, people are stepping up to utilize that information in many different ways. With the Internet, we can access copies of rare historical documents, research abstracts from half a world away, and download classical works of literature. ...The entire *United States Code* is online, as are decisions of the United States Supreme Court... *Scientific American* is online...Strunk and White's *Elements of Style* and Plato's *Republic*. ...The Internet is not the end-all and be-all of life. People will still continue to read printed material... But the Internet is an unlikely instrument of America's intellectual salvation. After all, to anyone on-line, the Internet is a disappointing source of knowledge and education. It's disorganized, inefficient, unreliable, and full of mindless trash." (Written by Ellen Beldner for *The Tartan,* Carnegie Mellon University, 24 February 1997). Another student from CMU, Joshua Walstrom, said: "Everyday the Web reorganizes itself. Old sites disappear, and new ones take their place...Search engines aren't helpful either. Try weeding out the data you need when your search engine returns 100,000 possible sites. You'd have better luck with a Ouija board."

The chapters in this book provide a means to take you and your students on a successful research journey to the Internet. You will find useful information on the correct strategies for searching diverse types of information and tested exercises to assist students in acquiring the necessary research skills for a rapidly expanding medium.

Unmasking the Internet for Research Using Hands-on Active Learning Exercises provides 18 lesson plans contributed by 23 librarians from different institutions across the United States. The chapters include the reasons for which the lesson plan was developed at each author's institution, the learning objectives, components of the in-class instruction, handouts distributed to classes, hands-on exercises or student activities, evaluation, and suggestions for teaching variations. Some special bibliographies are included, such as the Bibliography of WWW Sites Related to Web Instruction in the chapter "World Wide Web Navigation; Teaching Small Groups in 50 Minutes Using Hands-on Exercises" by the Texas A&M Libraries Web Instruction Team. The HTML documentation for three web tutorials is provided as well.

A special note: As of April 15, 1997, the URLs mentioned in the chapters were valid. Because changes occur so quickly, it is essential that each of them be verified before they are used in a teaching situation.

The book has been divided into four sections as indicated in the contents:
- Search Strategies to Navigate the Internet Successfully
- Search Strategies plus HTML for Web-Based Lessons
- Evaluation of Internet Sites
- Topic Oriented Internet Navigation

In order for the teaching librarians to utilize this book effectively, the activity or exercise sheets can be photocopied and distributed to their students. The activities are also available on disk for either the Windows environment or the Macintosh; the software used is Microsoft WORD. The advantage of the disk is that each library can then modify the activities and make any substitutions to fit their local situation. And of course, update the URLs.

The chapters of this book will be appropriate and useful not only at the college or university level but also for junior college and upper-level high school students who need to make efficient use of the variety of information on the Internet. We are told by educators that people learn best when they are involved in active learning, in their own style and at their own pace. One excellent way to help achieve learning is to provide a structured opportunity to "experience" information seeking on the Internet.

I want to especially thank the contributing authors for sharing their library instruction lesson plans. I also wish to express my gratitude to Dr. Rush Miller, Director of the University Library System at the University of Pittsburgh for his encouragement and support.

Librarians are urged to contact me with their suggestions for making this series of books more useful to them and their students. The first book in the Active Learning Series is entitled *"Empowering Students; Hands-on Library Instruction Activities."* Future books which are being planned will cover area studies, government publications, basic reference tools, and resources of art, music, and literature.

Marilyn P. Whitmore
Editor, Library Instruction Publications
222 Lytton Avenue
Pittsburgh, PA 15213-1410
mpw+@pitt.edu

Meet the Contributing Authors

Ruth J. Byers is Reference Librarian and Professor, Community College of Allegheny County, Pittsburgh PA. She was formerly Head of the Reference Dept., York County Library, Rock Hill, SC. Ruth received her BA, MLS and Certificate of Advanced Studies from the University of Pittsburgh. Email at rbyers@library.ccac.edu

John J. Burke is a reference librarian and Internet trainer at Fairmont State College in Fairmont, WV. He has published an article in Research Strategies entitled "Using E-mail to Teach: Expanding the Reach of BI" and *Learning the Internet: A Workbook for Beginners* (Neal-Schuman Publishers). He earned his MSLS from the University of Tennessee at Knoxville. Email at u536a@wvnvm.wvnet.edu

Elizabeth W. Carter is Assistant Professor and Information Services Librarian at The Citadel, Charleston, SC where she coordinates the library instruction program. Her areas of research are integration of library instruction into the college curriculum, and assessment of library instruction. She hold a BA degree in art history from Agnes Scott College and a M.L.S. from Emory University. Email at carter@Citadel.edu

Emaly Conerly is the Assistant Department Head of Circulation at Florida State University. Previously she was the Education Librarian at the University of Tennessee. She has also worked as a catalog librarian in academic libraries and a Coordinator of Children's Services in a county public library system. Emaly received her MLS from Emory University.

Barbara L. Cressman is Acting Reference Instruction Coordinator and Assistant Professor at the University of Illinois Libraries. She received an MM in music from Yale University and an MLIS at the University of Illinois. Barbara is active with the LIRT Computer Applications and IS Teaching Methods Committees and will be presenting a poster session on using the Internet for reference at ALA. She is authoring a chapter about planning new services in *Managing the Integration of Traditional and Electronic Resources* to be published in 1997. Email at cressman@ux1.cso.uiuc.edu

Katherine C. Ehrlich is an Information Researcher at the firm of Ernst & Young, LLP, Cleveland, Ohio. Previously she was the Reference Librarian at Katz Graduate School of Business, University of Pittsburgh. Ms. Ehrlich earned the MLS at the University of Pittsburgh and the BA at the University of Colorado. Email at Katherine.Ehrlich@ey.com

Bruce Harley is an Associate Librarian in the Government Publications & Maps Division of the San Diego State University Library. He is the Library's Coordinator of Electronic Information Services, in which role he has had primary responsibility for the Library's Internet instructional program since Spring, 1994. He also serves on the committee that oversees the development of the Library's WWW site (Libweb) @ http://libweb.sdsu.edu/ and is the primary author of the government information documents on Libweb. Email at harley@mail.sdsu.edu

Marcia King-Blandford is a Reference Librarian and serves as the Instruction Coordinator for the Information and Instruction Services Division at the Carlson Library, University of Toledo. She is Chair of the LIRT Program for the '97 ALA conference and also Chair of the '97 OHIONET Conference Program. Marcia is Co-Chair of the ACRL-STS General Discussion Group. Email at mkingbl@utnet.utoledo.edu

Janet McNeil Hurlbert is the Head of Instructional Services for the Snowden Library at Lycoming College. She received a BA in history and an MLS from the University of Denver. Janet has co-authored several articles with teaching colleagues on library instruction and serves as chair of the Teaching Effectiveness Committee for the college. Email at hurlbjan@lycoming.edu

Thura R. Mack has been a librarian at the University of Tennessee-Knoxville for ten years and has been the library liaison for Women's Studies (ten years) and Education (five years). She has authored many articles, including biographical essays, reviews, and scholarly research projects. Thura has been a presenter at various state, regional, and national conferences, including ALA, ACRL, Tennessee Library Association, Southeastern Library Association. She received her MLS from the University of Tennessee-Knoxville. Email at Thura-Mack@utk.edu

Pixey Anne Mosley is an Assistant Professor and the Senior Instructional Services Librarian for Evans Library at Texas A&M University. She is especially involved with outreach activities relating to library instruction. Her MLIS is from Louisiana State University; her pre-library background includes BS and MS degrees in Aerospace Engineering. Email at pmosley@tamu.edu

Necia Parker-Gibson is Library Instruction Coordinator at the University of Arkansas, Fayetteville. She has made numerous library instruction presentations on the local, regional, and national level and has published articles in *Research Strategies* and *College Teaching*. Necia's BS in Agriculture and MLIS are from Louisiana State University. Email at neciap@comp.uark.edu

Ann Perbohner is Information Services Manager with Research Access, Inc. in Pittsburgh. She has worked in automated services departments in both academic and public libraries. Her BA is from Shimer College and she will be receiving the MLIS from the University of Pittsburgh in 1997. Email at annp@netservices.com

Linda Ross is a research consultant on subjects including the development of expertise; the relationship between instructional design and cognition; and personal ethics. She received a Ph.D., with Honors, from the University of Illinois in Educational Psychology

Gail M. Staines is currently Coordinator of Library Instruction at Niagara County Community College, Sanborn, NY. She holds the MLS and a PhD in Higher Education Administration from the University of Buffalo where she is also an adjunct Assistant Professor. Gail is a library instruction consultant and guest speaker and was selected to be on the first list of ACRL's Information Literacy Advisors. Gail is the author of several articles. Email at staines@alpha.sunyniagara.cc.ny.us

Ru Story-Huffman is the Public Services Librarian at Cumberland College in Williamsburg, KY. She has worked in public libraries and as a adjunct instructor of children's literature. Ru is a workshop presenter, consultant in children's literature, and the author of *NURSERY RHYME TIME*, published by Highsmith Press. She has contributed to a number of educational journals and is a book reviewer for *Library Journal* and *LIBRES* electronic journal. Email at rshuff@cc.cumber.edu.

Texas A&M Libraries Web Instruction Team. Ann P. Daily is Reference and Instruction Librarian; Elaine Gass is Asst. Instructional Services Librarian; Judith K. Hart is Science Reference Librarian; Sharon K. Sandall is Business Reference Librarian; and Daniel Yi Ziao is Asst. Head, Electronic Reference Services Librarian.

Irene Weiner is the Reference and Instruction Librarian for the School of Professional and Graduate Studies at Baker University in Baldwin City, KS. She has worked in academic libraries at both the community college and university level where she has participated in an active program of library related public relations programs, one of which was the recipient of a Special John Cotton Dana Award. Irene received her BA and MLS degrees from UCLA. She is active in the ACRL and RUSA divisions of ALA and has made numerous presentations on library instruction issues. Email at iweiner@aol.com

Marilyn P. Whitmore is Editor of Library Instruction Publications and former Coordinator of Library Instruction in the University of Pittsburgh Libraries, 1984–1995. She has been active in ALA, especially the units dealing with instruction, collections development, and international library issues. Marilyn is the author of numerous publications. She holds the MLS from Rutgers University and PhD from the University of Pittsburgh. Contact by E-mail is: mpw+@pitt.edu

Integrating the Internet into Course-Related Instruction

PIXEY ANNE MOSLEY

Senior Instructional Services Librarian
EVANS LIBRARY, TEXAS A&M UNIVERSITY

Circumstances for the Instruction:

Many academic and school libraries integrate library instruction into coursework on a point-of-need basis. This usually involves students attending one or two 50-minute class sessions directed toward a variety of library resources. The sessions are followed by a "Library Research Assignment," often prepared by the course instructor. This assignment may be focused toward learning library skills or subject specific knowledge, depending on the instructor and course objectives.

More and more course instructors want to include the Internet as a resource and ask for it to be added into their "routine" course related library instruction. Occasionally, the instructors may be following a new department-mandated objective and do not understand what is on the Internet or how it should be used. In these situations, librarians have an opportunity to act in a pivotal role and guide the instructor and students toward achievable exercises involving critical use of Internet resources.

This chapter suggests methods for a librarian to:
- incorporate the Internet into an already crowded 50-minute instructional session,
- identify areas of critical information that need to be taught,
- point out some pitfalls to avoid, and
- provide several sample Internet hands-on exercises.

The librarian can suggest these hands-on exercises to the instructor in lieu of a potentially disastrous assignment, such as simply telling the student to find a home page on a controversial issue like abortion. The hands-on exercises could also be used during a library instruction session where computer facilities are available and lengthier sessions are an option.

Objectives of the Instruction:

- Introduce students to a web browser and basic navigation techniques such as clicking on links and typing in a URL.
- Establish understanding of structure and composition of Internet resources.
- Demonstrate both ineffective and effective searching techniques on the World Wide Web (WWW).
- Emphasize critical thinking and evaluation of information found on the web.

- Provide a specific starting point or applicable technique for finding relevant information.

Components of the Instruction:

STRESS BASIC CONCEPTS When introducing a class to the Internet for research or academic purposes, it is more important to explain basic concepts than to spend the available time zipping from site to site. Due to an excess of media hype, many students and faculty seem to come into the session with the impression that EVERYTHING is on the Internet and that it is *free* to everyone. Furthermore, they tend to expect that nearly everything on the Internet is accurate and valuable information.

DISPEL THE MYSTIQUE As difficult as it seems, the first task of any lecture involving the Internet is to perform a reality check and dispel the mystique of the World Wide Web. Show & Tell is a great tool to use in accomplishing this objective and maintain the student's attention. Ask someone to name a recent bestseller or new novel that they have read, explain that the book is not available full-text on the WWW (no matter how hard they look). However, they will be able to find reviews of the book, short promotional summaries, and could even mail-order the book from a bookstore's homepage using a credit card.

MENTION COPYRIGHT ISSUES At this point, it is a good idea to briefly mention the copyright and commercialized aspects of the World Wide Web. However, be careful not to get sidetracked.

LOCATE RESEARCH MATERIALS The next topic to cover is locating material on the web. Again, it is advantageous for the student to realize that using a WWW search engine for a simple general search does not work well. Go into one of the more extensive search engines (such as Alta Vista or HotBot) and ask someone from the class to provide a hobby, interest, or favorite TV/music personality. Generally, the results will be an overwhelming number of hits and going into two or three will quickly emphasize the non-academic nature of many sites. Now that the student has seen the scatter effect in action, librarians can emphasize some techniques for students to use in finding useful information for their coursework.

IDENTIFY SITES TO EXPLORE For subject-based course instruction, providing the student with some starter sites to explore is extremely helpful. Often one good site will link to another, especially when the web site is academic or government based.

UTILIZE THE LOCAL LIBRARY'S WEB SITE Additionally, the students are strongly encouraged to seek information from the Library's web site as an increasing number of connections are being provided to electronic databases, full-text journals, and government informational sources via hypertext links. This site also offers extensive resources focused toward self-improvement of library skills.

If your library has not developed a strong web site, refer the students to good homepages of other libraries in the region. Have several URLs selected and ready to share with the students in the class.

COMPUTER ACCESS ON CAMPUS Finally, it is important to tell students where and when they can find computers with WWW access and who they can contact for assistance. Even students who are familiar with the Internet from prior coursework may be unaware of more convenient library facilities and the type of searching expertise available from service desks.

REINFORCE RELATIONSHIPS A simple statement will serve to reinforce connectivity between the traditional term "LIBRARY" and the more innovative "INTERNET" or "WORLD WIDE WEB."

Handouts

If any handouts on using the Internet are available, they should be given out to the students. This is especially important since one of the key aspects of the World Wide Web is its remote accessibility. One handout that was developed by a fellow librarian and is used at Texas A&M University provides information on using some of the major search engines or Internet subject guides, such as Yahoo. The handout contents were reformatted and are accessible at the URL http://www.tamu.edu/library/reference/ handouts/netsrch.html. Such handouts should be kept simple as they will need to be updated frequently.

It is strongly recommended that the students be provided with a prepared paper handout listing the previously mentioned starter URL addresses. It is extremely disruptive for the student to frantically try to locate pen and paper and copy down a lengthy URL from the projected computer screen image or as it is recited. Valuable time is also lost with the repeated queries on punctuation and spelling. If the list of starter URLs is fairly short, consider economizing on paper by using a paper cutter and handing out half-sheets or quarter-sheet slips. Similarly, it is better to provide a longer list of complete URLs than to just provide a URL for the starting point and start clicking away through several layers of links.

Make copies of screen prints of "busier" or important web pages. They provide the student with the exact URL and provide space for the student to make notes and annotations regarding specific hypertext links, etc. This type of handout is quick and easy to produce. The primary drawback comes from paper costs for covering a large number of web sites or if the class itself is quite large.

Hands-on Assignments:

Three models of basic, intermediate, and advanced follow-up hands-on assignments are included and can be used as templates. Other librarians can modify the subject areas, the URL addresses, or the scope based on particular course objectives, available computer resources, and time expectations.

The ideal is to build Web location skills while incorporating
> critical thinking,
> summarization, and
> evaluation skills.

The hands-on assignments have been presented on separate sheets so that librarians may easily customize them with the activities disk.

Evaluation

Formal or informal evaluative techniques can be used for this style of instruction. Follow-up, post-assignment feedback can be obtained by administering a survey to the class or by evaluating the quality of the completed assignments.

Alternately, the librarian can meet with the instructor and/or arrange to visit the class initiating discussion-based feedback. Unfortunately, these feedback mechanisms are dependent on the cooperation of the course instructor and may not be available in all cases.

Basic Hands-on Assignment

Introducing the student to the Internet and browser. Specific URLs are provided.

Step 1   Locate and contrast the following three web sites for a two-page paper. Discuss the size/depth of the web site, the type of information provided, and how the information is presented.

http://www.nasa.gov
http://——(insert the URL for a site of a current hit movie review)
http://www.cnn.com

Step 2   Consult the Virtual Library Tour
http://www.tamu.edu/library/reference/virtual/tour00.html and

the online library handout on finding periodical articles
http://www.tamu.edu/library/reference/handouts/serials.html
to answer the following questions.
Note to librarians. Follow with several library skills questions answerable from the identified web pages. Here are examples:

What is the name of the library's online catalog?_____
What materials are located on the numbered partition tables in the reference area?_____
What is the name of the area that contains the most recent issues of magazines newspapers?_____

Step 3   Use the Alta Vista search engine http://altavista.digital.com/ to locate a homepage for the Phoenix Chamber of Commerce in Arizona. Provide the
URL   of the homepage and describe the information you found on it.

_____

_____

_____

Intermediate Hands-on Assignment

More search skills and comprehension of the terminology are required on the part of the searcher.

Step 1   Write a 500 word review of the following electronically published article accessible from the library's web site.

CITATION: Fidler, David P. "Globalization, International Law, and Emerging Infectious Diseases," *Emerging Infectious Diseases*, 2:2 (April-June 1996).

Attach the review to this sheet.

Step 2   In approximately 500 words, compare and contrast the University's electronic *PHONBOOK* option to the paper copy of the Student/Faculty/Staff Directory available at the Information Desk.

Attach your comparison to this sheet.

Step 3   Locate and briefly describe 3 separate web sites that include information about rain forest conservation efforts. Rate the value of the information from the web site on a scale of 1-5 (5 is highly useful, 1 is useless). In a paragraph (less than 1 page) explain why you rated each site as you did; attach your description to this sheet.

Student..

Advanced Hands-on Assignment

This assignment requires significant judgment and initiative skills from the student. It involves the comprehensive coverage of a web site.

Step 1   Determine if the following information is available from the Hewlett-Packard Corporate web site http://www.hp.com. Provide the specific URLs used to answer the questions.
Note to librarians. Select exercises for the students which will require them to identify specific information such as CEO, Mission Statement, Product lines, Press releases, etc.

Step 2   Locate and compare a private, academic, and government web site disseminating information on Equal Rights issues.

Step 3   Contrast the effectiveness of using Alta Vista, WebCrawler, and Yahoo to locate material available from the Center for Disease Control regarding the Ebola virus.
Discuss the type and quantity of material retrieved by each technique. Your paper should be four pages double-spaced.

Notes:

Netscape; An Introduction and Advanced Search Strategies

RUTH J. BYERS

Reference Librarian & Professor
COMMUNITY COLLEGE OF ALLEGHENY COUNTY, PITTSBURGH, PA

Circumstances for the Instruction Sessions:

LIBRARY INSTRUCTION PROGRAM: Statement of Purpose

The Community College of Allegheny County (CCAC) is committed to providing an accessible and affordable college education, greater educational opportunity, comprehensive college programming, and quality instruction in the classroom. In keeping with that commitment, the Library offers a variety of instructional sessions. These sessions were created to support the goal of the College to develop the skills in all students to become confident, independent learners and capable problem solvers.

To meet the challenge of effectively teaching students how to use the Library's new electronic resources to conduct research, we have expanded our Library Instruction Program to include a series of resource-specific sessions that can be used in place of, or to supplement, our traditional course-related library instruction.

NETSCAPE; AN INTRODUCTION and NETSCAPE; ADVANCED SEARCH STRATEGIES

Purpose:

To introduce the use of Netscape and the Internet for research with emphasis on search strategy in the advanced session. The Netscape sessions supplement other academic course offerings on the Internet by focusing on the Internet as one tool within the broader context of library research.

Content:

Netscape; An Introduction was designed for students with little or no exposure to Netscape and the Internet. Students learn the basic features of Netscape as a means of accessing and using the Internet.

Netscape; Advanced Search Strategies was designed so that students learn what it means to develop a search strategy for research on the Internet. They learn to apply it for research on the Internet using different Web search engines.

Objectives of the instruction:

Upon completion of both library instruction sessions:
- Students will be familiar with the Netscape browser and its features.
- Students will successfully navigate the Internet using Netscape.
- Students will formulate search strategies for research topics and apply them to Internet searches.
- Students will evaluate information retrieved through the Internet searching.

Components of the Library Instruction:

These sessions were designed to be used as stand-alone modules that could be offered to students on an open enrollment basis. They are flexible enough, however, to also be used as modules in course-related instruction programs.

Each session, Introduction and Advanced, is for one 50-minute or one 75-minute time block. Each module contains a presentation outline to be used with accompanying PowerPoint slides or an overhead projector and the live Netscape demonstration. We have included notes for presenters to help ensure consistency among library instructors. The outline also includes references to the handouts prepared for the session. The handouts are included in this chapter.

We use two direct projection units for these classes, one for the live Netscape demo and the other to show the accompanying PowerPoint slides that introduce and illustrate the various concepts. We have also given this program with just one projector, toggling back and forth in Windows (Alt-Tab) between Netscape and PowerPoint. We have also used an LCD panel with an overhead projector for Netscape, and a second overhead for the slides. It would be very easy to put the information on transparencies and project them for the class if the equipment or software mentioned above is not available.

Adaptation for Faculty Instruction:

These modules can also be adapted for faculty instruction. Time and topics can be adapted to meet the needs of the target audience. Finding lesson plans for different subject areas makes a good demonstration topic in faculty sessions.

Netscape; An Introduction
Presentation Outline

Note that NET—refers to live actions in Netscape

Projection 1: Introductory

Name of college/university
Class name and library instruction session

- Netscape: Introduction

Projection 2: Goals

- Learn the basics of using Netscape to navigate the Internet
- Learn the Yahoo search engine

Projection 3: Library Research Steps

- Where does the Internet fit?
- When to use the Internet?
    Point out that rarely is it the best first step in research process
        Give a couple of examples where:
        Need very current information
        Event in progress
        Latest research
        Topic frequently updated i.e. weather, stock quotes, headline news
    Point out that it is best to use this as only one of the steps
        Don't overlook or omit other sources
        Consult with a librarian if unsure when to use

Projection 4: Definitions

- What is the Internet?
- What is the WWW?
- What is a browser?
- What is Netscape?
    Point out that it is very important to evaluate material obtained on the Internet
    because it is a vast, uncontrolled format—on anything, from anyone.
    Briefly define each term; set the scene.
    Refer to the Internet Glossary handout for definitions of term.

Projection 5: NET—Home Pages

CCAC Home Page

- What is a Home Page?
  - Briefly define
    - Refer again to Internet Glossary handout
    - Mention that this is the **default home page** when accessing Netscape from CCAC Computing Suite
- Navigational basic is the **mouse**
  - Ask how many are "mouse literate"
  - Point out **links**, especially how to recognize them
  - Point out **Back/Forward/Stop** on Toolbar
    - Briefly define purpose
    - Refer to Netscape Toolbar/Directory Buttons handout (included in this   chapter)

HANDS-ON—Go to Library System Home Page

Have students select one of several ways to connect from this page

Projection 6: NET—Home Pages

LIBRARY SYSTEM HOME PAGE

Hands on —Scroll down; briefly review

Go to the **Allegheny** page

Have students click on this

ALLEGHENY CAMPUS LIBRARY HOME PAGE

Mention that this is the **default home page** when accessing Netscape from CCAC Library

Point out different **links**

Hands on —Scroll down

SEARCH ENGINES

Tools to let you search by topic

INTERNET ASSIGNMENT PAGES

Show but do not connect

SELECTED INTERNET RESOURCES

Show but do not connect

Projection 7: NET—Toolbar/Buttons

- Briefly review
- **Demonstrate** how to access **Handbook** and why
  - Point out contents and index
- Refer again to the Netscape Toolbar/Directory Buttons handout
- **Go Back** to Allegheny Library Home Page using **BACK** from Toolbar

Projection 8: NET—Toolbar/Buttons

- What's New
- What's "Cool"
    Briefly explain both
    Note date updated
    HANDS ON —pick a site and connect
    Poll students for their selections

Projection 9: PPT—URLs

- Universal Resource Locator
- The "address" of a Web page
        Example: www.disney.com
- The "path" to a Web page

Projection 10: URLs

- Types of sites:

.com	Commercial	www.cbs.com
.edu	Educational	www.pitt.edu
.gov	Governmental	www.whitehouse.gov
.org	Organizational	www.aclu.org

    Mention that this format sometimes can be used to guess at addresses
    Refer them to *URL* handout for more examples and information

Projection 11: NET—Open an URL

- Point out **OPEN** from the Toolbar
        HANDS ON—Use a URL from the URL handout
        Have students keep a site on the screen

Projection 12: NET—Toolbar/Buttons

- Bookmarks—Demo
        Briefly define
        Explain window options

HANDS ON—have the class **ADD** one for the page on screen
- View Bookmarks
        Close Bookmarks

Projection 13: Net—Print Demo

- Print preview—Demonstrate
    Explain how to access from **FILE**
    Explain where to look for number of pages in document
    Cancel and select **FILE** again
    Select **PRINT** and explain window options
    Cancel

Projection 14: Net—Download

HANDS ON—Click on FILE
    Point out Save As
        Briefly define
- Select SAVE AS from the menu
    Explain window options
        DRIVE: select A
        TYPE
        FILE NAME
- Download one page from last site

Projection 15: Search Engines

- Navigational tool
- Search the Web by topic
    Point out Internet Glossary handout again
    Searching/Search Engine class
        Mention that there will be a second Internet class offered that will deal solely with
            Searching and Search Engines
        Discuss schedule and registration information available in their packet

Projection 16: NET—Open Practice

HANDS ON
Have the students practice by connecting to sites in *What's Cool* or *What's New,* use URLs,
follow links on Home Pages, or experiment with Search Engines

Projection 17: Review the Goals

Learn the basic of using Netscape to navigate the Internet

Learn the Yahoo search engine

Netscape: Advanced Search Strategies

Projection 1: Introduction

Name of college/university
Class name and library instruction session
- Netscape: Advanced Search Strategies
    Search Strategy
    Search Engines

Projection 2: Goals

- Value of the Internet for research
- Develop a search strategy
- Apply the strategy to search engines

Projection 3: Library Research

Where does the Internet fit?
When to use the Internet?

Point out that it is rarely the best first step in the research process
    Give examples of where it might be:
        Need very current information
        Event in progress
        Topic frequently updated, e.g. weather, stock quotes, headline news
Point out is best to use this as only one of the research steps
    Don't overlook or omit other sources
    Consult with the Librarian if unsure when to use
Point out the need to evaluate information found on the Internet

Projection 4: Search Strategy: Think before you search!

- Think through your search
- Ask yourself questions
- Find words to search

Projection 5: Search Strategy Worksheet

- Select a topic
    State it as clearly & completely, for example:
        HOW TEENS CAN PREVENT AIDS
- Pick out the main concepts or keywords
- Think of synonyms for each keyword

Note: At CCAC, we use this example as a **good example** of a multi-faceted social issues topic. The topic can be changed to illustrate other subject areas or faculty assignments.

Projection 6: Search Strategy Worksheet

- **HOW TEENS CAN PREVENT AIDS**
- Keywords:
    AIDS or **Acquired Immune Deficiency Syndrome** or **HIV**
    Teens or **Teenagers** or **Adolescents**
    Prevent or **Prevention**

Projection 7: Mix and Match your Keywords

- Different combinations to express your search:

AIDS	teens	prevent
AIDS	teenagers	prevent
AIDS	adolescents	prevention
AIDS	teens or adolescents	prevention

Projection 8: Truncation Broadens your Search

- Search several versions of a word at the same time:
    prevent? or prevent* finds:
        prevent
        prevents
        preventing
        prevention
    Symbols may vary in different search engines
    Not all search engines allow truncation
    Some *assume* truncation

Projection 9: Final Search Strategy

- AIDS   teen* or adolescen*   prevent*
        One example of a search strategy from selected keywords

    Explain that some search engines will enable you to enter your combinations more efficiently than others

Projection 10: Search Engines—Definition

- Navigational tool
- Search the Web by topic
    Mention the *Search Engine* handouts

Projection 11: Search Engines—Types

- Hierarchical **or** Directories
- Form-based **or** Indexes
- Combinations

Projection 12: A Hierarchical Search Engine

YAHOO

- Levels of topics
- More focused at each level
- Ends with list of sites

Projection 13: Form-based Search Engine Alta Vista

- Type in search
- Provides list of sites
    Emphasize importance of reading Help
    Mention handout "WORLD WIDE WEB SEARCH ENGINES: SEARCH FEATURES"
    Point out that each search engine is different

Projection 14: Search Strategy

- How teens can prevent AIDS
- AIDS   teen* or adolescen*   prevent*

Projection 15: NET—Connect to Search Engines

- Go to the Library System or Allegheny Campus Library Home Page
- Link to the *WEB SEARCH ENGINES* page
    Briefly review contents of page
    Review general and topical search engines and what they cover
        Note: Search engines can also be accessed from the NetSearch Directory Button in
        Netscape
    Refer to the handout "World Wide Web Search Engines: Search Features:"

Projection 16: NET—Alta Vista

HANDS ON—Link to the *Alta Vista* search engine
> Point out the "advanced search" choice, but use the "simple" for this exercise
> Select **Help**
> Emphasize the importance of viewing **Help** when using a new search engine
> Use **Help** to formulate a search based on selected search strategy

INTERACTIVE—encourage students to help shape the search

Projection 17: NET—Alta Vista - Case Sensitivity

- Find the section on CAPITAL LETTERS in HELP
> Point out why case sensitivity can be important
> **AIDS** vs. **aids**

Projection 18: Alta Vista - Case Sensitivity

- How teens can prevent AIDS
- AIDS   teen* or adolescen*   prevent*
- aids teen* or adolescen*   prevent*

Projection 19: Net—Alta Vista - Forced Inclusion/Exclusion

- Find in **Help** the section on **Forced inclusion/exclusion**
> From our search example, what words do we want to include?
> > AIDS   prevention   teenagers or adolescents
> Does Alta Vista provide a way to ask for synonyms?
> > Can we use "or"?
> > > NO. Not in Simple search; Advanced Search will allow its use.
> > > We must do two searches to use both terms (teenagers or adolescents).

Projection 20: Alta Vista - Forced Inclusion

- How teens can prevent AIDS
- AIDS teen* or adolescen* prevent*
> AIDS+teenager+prevention
> AIDS+adolescent+prevention
> + is the symbol in Alta Vista for Forced Inclusion
> **+ tells Alta Vista that the word following must be included**

Projection 21: NET—ALTA VISTA - Truncation

Stay in HELP and SCROLL down and find Truncation
> Can we use a symbol to expand a word? Yes, use *

Projection 22: Alta Vista - Truncation

- teen*   adolescen*   prevent*
- teenS   adolescenCE   preventS
- teenAGER   adolescenT   preventING
- teenAGERS   adolescenTS   prevenTION

Projection 23: Alta Vista - Truncation

How teens can prevent AIDS
AIDS+teen*+prevent*
AIDS+adolescen*+prevent*

Projection 24: NET—Alta Vista - Enter Search

Hands-on
> Have students enter either search and link to some of sites retrieved
> Presenter also run one of the searches
> Poll a few students about results
> Point out the importance of evaluating the sites and results

Projection 25: Evaluating Search Results

- Who produced or authored the document?
- Are they representing any particular institution or group?
  > Bias?
- Is the information **fact or personal opinion**?
  > Research?
  > Comments, letters?

Projection 26: NET—Alta Vista "Live Topics"

- Use to focus results of search
- Extracts keywords from results
- Groups keywords and secondary terms based on results of search
- Choose only a few to include or exclude in each round of revision
  > Demonstrate once or twice
  > Poll group for results
- Reiterate evaluation of sites

Projection 27: Citing Web Resources

- APA Format
- MLA Format

> Mention that both are included on handouts "Citing Electronic Resources…"

World Wide Web Search Engines: Search Features

Most World Wide Web search engines let you fine-tune your search using some of the following methods. The terms and examples used here are generic and don't represent any particular search engine. Each search engine is different. Many have a simple or basic level and an advanced level. Read the online help of the search engines you use. If you have any questions about search features or the terminology used to describe them, please ask for assistance at your campus library's Reference Desk.

How Search Engines Treat Words

Keyword searching
All search engines use keyword searching. This means you use your own words to run the search. This is powerful because the search engine will look for whatever you type in, but this is also a limitation—the search engine is only looking for the word. The word has no context or meaning. Therefore, time spent thinking through your topic, deciding how to focus your search, looking for alternate words to use in the search, and paying careful attention to the features listed below will pay off in much more useful results.

Capitalization
Some search engines are case sensitive. This means they treat capital letters (upper case) differently from small letters (lower case). Usually it's best to enter words or phrases in lower case. Capitalizing a word often narrows the search.

Example—turkey
Finds pages about the bird and the country.
Example—Turkey
Finds pages about the country but not about the bird.

Truncation
Truncation lets you use part of a word to search several variations of the word at the same time. This is often indicated by an asterisk, but a different symbol, such as a question mark, might be used.

Example: colleg*
This will look for collegE, collegES, collegIAL, collegIATE, etc.)

Beware of automatic truncation. Some search engines truncate words automatically unless you tell it not to. This can lead to many false hits (web pages not relevant to your needs).

Combining Words

Usually you will want to use more than one word in your search. This helps to focus your topic. Capitalization and truncation can be used when combining words.

Finding two or more words in one search

When you enter two or more words, most search engines assume you want to find web pages that contain all of the words.

Example: dogs cats iguanas

Often the search engine will rank the results of a search entered as shown in the example above. This means that it will list web pages that have all three words first, then those that have two of the words, then those that have only one of the words. See forced inclusion and term matching for ways to eliminate the pages with only one or two search words.

Some search engines expect you to tell them that you want them to find all of the words. This is usually done by including the word between your search words. Some search engines use a symbol such as +. ↓"and"

Example: dogs and cats and iguanas
          dogs +cats +iguanas

Additional specialized ways to find ~~for~~ two or more words at once are:

Phrase searching

This asks the search engine to find a phrase exactly as you enter it. A phrase is often indicated with quotation marks, but some search engines use other symbols, such as underscores, to link words into phrases.

Example: "state of the union"
          state_of_the_union

A variation of phrase searching, called proximity searching, lets you indicate that words (or phrases) must be close to each other, but not necessarily next to each other as in an exact phrase. Sometimes you can specify the maximum amount of separation by number of words or number of characters.

Forced inclusion

This specifies that a word or phrase must be included in the results.

Example: +cats dogs iguanas

The results must include the word "cats." They may or may not include the words "dogs" or "iguanas."

Forced exclusion

The opposite of forced inclusion, forced exclusion specifies that a word or phrase cannot be part of the result. This may be indicated by a symbol, such as "-" or by the word "not."

Example: cats iguanas-dogs
          cats iguanas not dogs

The results may include the words "cats" or "iguanas," but sites with the words "dogs" will be excluded from the results.

Term matching

This lets you indicate the number of your search words or phrases that must be matched without specifying which ones must be matched.

      Example: cats dogs iguanas boas pets [match 3 terms]

Each result must include any three of your search terms.

Boolean Operators (AND, OR, NOT)

Finding two or more words in a single search, forced inclusion, forced exclusion, and "Or" are actually the Boolean operators *and*, *or* and *not* as shown in the examples. These are logical operators were named after the nineteenth-century English logician, George Boole. Some search engines will indicate the Boolean operators together as a single feature rather than listing them separately as shown above.

Nesting

Nesting is usually associated with Boolean operators and generally uses parentheses to combine several features in a single search.

      Example: (cats OR dogs) AND (iguanas OR boas)

Results must include either the word "cats" or the word "dogs" and must also include the word "iguanas" or the word "boas."

Finding Alternate Words

Often in addition to combining words, you may want to the search engine to look for two or more different words that mean the same thing (synonyms) or alternate words that represent different ways to think about your topic. You must tell the search engine that you don't want it to find pages with all of the words, but pages with any one of the words is OK.

"OR"

In most cases, using the word "or" between synonyms or alternate words will tell the search engine that you want to find pages with any one of the words. Some search engines use a symbol, such as "|" to do this.

      Example: cats or dogs or iguanas

             cats | dogs | iguanas

Other Options

Directed Searches: Some search engines let you specify which web page elements to search or what type of Internet resource to look for.

      Page elements: URLs (links), host name, summaries, or complete page.

      Types of resources: Web pages, gopher sites, Usenet News, ftp sites, telnet sites.

Weighted searches, ranking and relevancy

Most search engines automatically rank the results in some way (also referred to as relevancy or weighting>). This means they list sites that most closely match your search at the top of the list of results. How the search engine does this can have a significant effect on the results. Some provide an explanation of the method they use; most do not. Some let you determine how results are ranked in one of the ways given here.

Weighted search words or phrases: Search engines with this feature let you specify a degree of importance or relevancy of a word or phrase.

Weighted results: This feature gives you some control over how the search engine ranks the results of your search. An example might be to tell the search engine to rank pages that contain your word in the title of the page higher than those that contain your word somewhere in the body of the page.

Limiting (filtering): Where allowed, this feature lets you refine the results of your search by running a second search against the results of your first search. You can generally use all the search features that the search engine provides, but you will be searching only those sites that were returned by your original search.

Formatting results: Some search engines let you format the results of the search. This is usually a choice among types of display, such as standard, detailed, etc. You can often specify the number of items you want to see.

Evaluating Sites & Evaluating Search Engines

As the Internet grows, it becomes increasingly important to learn and use the features of search engines to focus your search and get useful results. Some search engines help you narrow your search before you begin.

Evaluation (site reviews: Search engines that evaluate web sites let you limit the search to only those sites that have been evaluated or reviewed. This often provides much better results than searching the entire web indiscriminately.

Topical search engines: Sometimes called limited area search engines, or LASEs, topical search engines only search for web pages on a particular topic. An example is a search engine that only looks for career resources, or one that focuses on art. These specialized search engines are becoming more common as the Internet continues to grow.

Text by David Mooney
Allegheny Campus Library 1996

CITING ELECTRONIC RESOURCES
APA: AMERICAN PSYCHOLOGICAL ASSOCIATION STYLE

INTERNET

Form: Author's Last Name, Initial of First Name (date). *Title of work.* [Document type]. URL (date visited)
   ["Date visited" is optional. Use "URL" where appropriate]

Examples: **World Wide Web Document:**
Beckleheimer, J. (1994). *How do you cite URLs in a bibliography?* [WWW document]. URL http://www.nrlssc.navy.mil/meta/bibliography.html (1996, December 6)

Newsgroup & Listserv Postings
Seabrook, Richard H.C. (1994, January 22) *Community and Progress.* [On-line news posting]. cybermind@jefferson.village.virginia.edu

Reference: Land, T. (1996, November 3). *Web extension to American Psychological Association style (WEAPAS) (Rev. 1.3.3).* [WWW document]. http://www.nyu.edu/pages/psychology/WEAPAS/

OTHER ELECTRONIC MEDIA

Form: Author's Last Name, Initial of First Name (date). Title of article. *Name of Periodical or Document* [Document or Service Type], pages. Available: Specify path (date visited)

Example: Cancer cases rise seen, deaths level. (1995, May 4). *Facts on FileWorld New Digest.* [CD-ROM], 323C2. Available: EBSCOfile: Facts on File World News Digest Item: 1995000029
   [When no author is given, list the title of the article first]

Pinto, J. K., Geiger, M. A. & Boyle, E. J. (1994, March). A three-year longitudinal study of changes in student learning styles. [On-line]. *Journal of College Student Development*, 35, 113-119. Abstract from File: PsychFirst Item: 81-47046

References: American Psychological Association. (1995). *Publication manual of the American Psychological Association* (4th ed.). Washington, DC: Author.

Li, Xia & Crane, Nancy B. (1993). *Electronic style: a guide to citing electronic information.* Westport, CT: Meckler.

CITING ELECTRONIC RESOURCES
MLA: MODERN LANGUAGE ASSOCIATION STYLE

INTERNET

Form: Author's Last Name, First Name. "Title of Work." *Title of Complete Work.* [Protocol and address] (Date of visit)
[Title of complete Work may not always be applicable]

Examples: **World Wide Web Document**

Beckleheimer, John. "How do you cite URLs in a bibliography?" http://www.nrlssc.navy.mil/meta/bibliography.html (6 Dec. 1996)

Newsgroup & Listserv Postings

Seabrook, Richard H. C. "Community and Progress." cybermind@jefferson.village.virginia.edu (6 Dec. 1996)

Reference: Walker, Janice R. "MLA-Style Citations of Electronic Sources (Endorsed by the Alliance for Computers & Writing)." http://www.cas.usf.edu/english/walker/mia.html (22 Nov. 1996).

OTHER ELECTRONIC MEDIA

Form: Author's Last Name, First Name. "Title of Article." *Title of original (print) source* Date of source: page number of source. *Title of Electronic Source.* Publication Medium. Name of Vendor. Electronic publication date.

Examples: "Cancer Cases Rise Seen, Deaths Level." *Facts on File World News Digest.* May 4, 1995: 323C2. *Facts on File World News Digest.* CD-ROM EBSCO. August, 1996.

Pinto, John K., et al. "A Three-year Longitudinal Study of Changes in Student Learning Styles." *Journal of college Student Development.* March, 1994: 113-119. *PsychFirst.* On-line. FirstSearch. April, 1994.

References: Gibaldi, Joseph. *MLA Handbook for Writers of Research Papers.* 4th ed.New York: Modern Language Association of America, 1995.

INTERNET GLOSSARY

BOOKMARKS

Method of marking & retrieving specific Web sites. Many Web browsers enable you to store the names and locations of interesting sites in bookmark collections. Using a bookmark is a great shortcut.

BROWSER

Software used for navigating the Web. Web browsers enable users to access the many kinds of information on the Web, such as text, graphics, video, and audio. Netscape is the most popular Web browser, followed by Microsoft's Explorer.

DOWNLOAD

To copy a file from a remote system to your computer.

FAQ (Frequently Asked Questions)

A file that contains a list of questions that are asked regularly and the answers to those questions. FAQs are used to prevent the same questions from being asked repeatedly by new users.

GOPHER

A menu-based Internet program used to find information in directories or files.

HOME PAGE

The first page you see when you access a Web site. Typically serves as an index or table of contents to other documents stored at the site.

INTERNET

A global communications system that links over three million computers. Internet users often refer to it as "The Net."

LISTSERV

A program used for handling mailing lists.

LOCAL AREA NETWORK (LAN)
A computer network linking a relatively small area such as a building or group of buildings.

LYNX
A character-based program for accessing the World Wide Web; a text browser.

NETSCAPE NAVIGATOR
A graphical browser for the WWW, often referred to as just "Netscape."

SEARCH ENGINE
A navigational tool to search the Web by topic.

TELNET
An Internet service that lets one computer act as the terminal for another.

URL (Universal Resource Locator)
Method for stating the address of things on the Web. URLs are case sensitive. They must be entered exactly as given.

WIDE AREA NETWORK (WAN)
A computer network linking a relatively large geographical area. A system of LANs connected.

WORLD WIDE WEB (WWW)
An Internet system of servers that supports documents formatted in HTML as well as links to other documents, graphics, audio, and video files. Also known as "The Web."

Allegheny Campus Library 1996

Netscape Assignment

Search Strategy Worksheet

Step 1   Select a topic.

_____

Step 2   State your topic as completely as you can:

_____

_____

_____

_____

Step 3   Think of different words that may be used to convey the same things.

Step 4   Write each word or concept in the spaces below.
Circle the most important.

           Concept 1   &   Concept 2   &   Concept 3

OR   _____   _____   _____

OR   _____   _____   _____

OR   _____   _____   _____

Step 5   Write your search strategy as you will type it.

_____

_____

_____

Teaching Faculty to Use the Internet as an *Effective* Research and Teaching Resource; An Interactive Approach

GAIL M. STAINES

Coordinator of Library Instruction
NIAGARA COUNTY COMMUNITY COLLEGE, SANBORN, NY

Circumstances for the Instruction Session:

Most Internet searchers are moving from the "newbie" stage to a stage of understanding about the information superhighway. Some are familiar with the history of the Internet. Some are proficient in using electronic mail, listservs, and newsgroups. Most find searching the Internet effectively for information a challenge. In responding to a needs assessment of faculty at the Niagara County Community College (NCCC), the *Teaching and Learning with Technology Series* (TLT) was created. The TLT series addresses academicians concerns of:

- how to locate information for research and teaching;
- how to evaluate information for credibility and reliability;
- how to cite information found in cyberspace.

Designing instruction to teach faculty how to use the Internet effectively required careful planning. Busy faculty schedules, limited Internet access, and a range of faculty computer experience were considered in instructional design.

Three workshops were created as part of the TLT series. Each workshop was designed to be 90 minutes in length. Interactive and experiential teaching techniques are used. Each session begins with what faculty know, and are familiar and comfortable with, in using the Internet. These sessions work best with a group of no more than 10 people. A second instructor or teaching assistant may be useful to act as a "roving" instructor—helping workshop participants with individual questions if more than 10 people are in the workshop.

Pre-registration is required for all workshops. This ensures that faculty enroll at the appropriate level of their Internet experience. For example, faculty who are comfortable with the Internet, but who do not know how to effectively search the 'Net for information, may skip Part I and enroll in Parts II and III. At pre-registration, faculty are also asked to bring topics which they may want to explore on the Internet.

Workshop I. Introduction to the Internet

The overall goal of the first workshop is for faculty at NCCC to understand Internet basics.

Objectives of Instruction:

Upon completion of this instruction session:
- Faculty are familiar with the history of the Internet.
- Faculty understand the equipment and software needed to access the Internet.
- Faculty understand Internet capabilities (e-mail, discussion groups, newsgroups, World Wide Web).
- Faculty are able to execute basic searching on a search engine.

Components of Instruction:

The overall goal of Workshop I is to provide an overview of the Internet. This introductory session enables faculty not familiar with the Internet to become so rather quickly. Teaching techniques used are lecture, discussion, demonstration, and hands-on experience.

Introduction and Overview (15 minutes):

The librarian outlines the goals and objectives of Workshop I. A brief overview of what the Internet is, the capabilities of the Internet, and access on campus and from home and office are discussed. Faculty are asked to share their Internet experiences. The videotape, *The Amazing Internet,* (Lancaster, PA : Classroom Connect, 1996, 20 minutes) is shown.

Equipment and Software (10 minutes):

An overview of equipment and software needed to access the Internet is presented.

Search Engines (10 minutes):

An introduction to search engines is given. The librarian conducts several sample searches on different search engines (such as Alta Vista, HotBot, Yahoo) to show varying results. Faculty are asked for topics which are used to demonstrate searches.

Hands-On Exploration (25 minutes):

Faculty are given time to explore the Internet search engines on their own. The librarian is available to answer any questions and facilitate discussion. Twenty-five minutes enables faculty to explore the 'Net at their leisure while taking into account 'Net activity which, at times, slows retrieval of information.

Conclusion (10 minutes):

The librarian reviews the session and answers any questions which faculty still pose. A separate workshop taught by Computer Center staff is offered to provide faculty with instruction on how to use e-mail. In this particular workshop, faculty set-up their own e-mail accounts.

Workshop II. Searching the Internet for Information Effectively

The overall goal is for faculty at NCCC to search the Internet effectively for information.

Objectives of the Instruction:

Upon completion of this instruction session:
- Faculty are able to create a research strategy using Boolean searching (and, or, not).
- Faculty are able to apply a search strategy to search engines.
- Faculty understand the differences between various search engines.
- Faculty understand controlled vocabulary searching and keyword searching.

Components of Instruction:

The overall goal of Workshop II is to teach faculty how to search the Internet effectively in order to locate information. It is assumed they have met the goal and objectives of Workshop I.

Introduction and Overview: (10 minutes)

The librarian explains the goals and objectives of Workshop II. Faculty are asked to share their Internet searching experiences and knowledge of Boolean searching. Each participant is also asked to share the topic they wish to explore on the Internet.

Research Strategy: (30 minutes)

The research process, including how to create a research strategy, is explained. Boolean searching (and, or, not) is presented. (A worksheet entitled "Research Strategy Worksheet" is included and can be photocopied.) Faculty use the worksheet provided to create their own research strategy on a particular topic. Controlled vocabulary searching is compared to keyword searching. The librarian demonstrates a search on the library's on-line catalog using controlled vocabulary. The MARC record is very briefly explained and is compared to hypertext language on a web page. One or two faculty searches are then used as examples.

Directories and Search Engines: (20 minutes)

Differences between searching a directory and searching a search engine are presented. A search using a directory, such as Yahoo http://www.yahoo.com is demonstrated. The same search is used to demonstrate a search engine. Any search engine can be used, such as Alta Vista http://www.altavista.digital.com, HotBot http://www.hotbot.com, or

WebCrawler http://webcrawler.com. A list of "Quick Internet Search Tips" is reviewed; a copy is included in this chapter and may be photocopied.

Hands-on Experience: (30 minutes)

Faculty are given time to explore the Internet search engines on their own. The librarian is available to answer any questions and facilitate discussion. Thirty minutes enables faculty to explore the 'Net at their leisure while taking into account 'Net activity which, at times, slows retrieval of information.

For more information, please see "Resources to Consult for Searching the Internet Effectively" in this chapter.

RESEARCH STRATEGY WORKSHEET

Your topic: ....

Develop a list of keywords with synonyms:
Circle the most important keywords in your topic.

	Concept 1		**Concept 2**		**Concept 3**
	_____	and	_____	and	_____
or					
	_____	and	_____	and	_____
or					
	_____	and	_____	and	_____

....
follow the example below to complete the exercise

EXAMPLE

Topic: What impact do pollutants have on Lakes Erie and Ontario in regards to fishing?

Keywords, with synonyms:

	Concept 1		**Concept 2**		**Concept 3**
	pollutants	and	Lake Erie	and	fishing
or					
	water pollution	and	Lake Ontario	and	sport fishing
or					
	PCBs	and	great lakes	and	bass

QUICK INTERNET SEARCH TIPS

When selecting a search engine to use consider:

> **size** of the search engine's database
> **content**
> **currency**
> **searching speed**
> **interface design**

Read the search engine's help screens and instructions; these change frequently.

Try phrasing your search in different ways.

Conduct your search using different search engines.

Search alternative spellings of words.
> e.g., theater———theatre

Try alternative keywords, synonyms.
> e.g., capital punishment———death penalty———executions

....

Know the http:// address. It's the quickest way to get to where you need to go.

If you do not know the http:// address, try:
> http://www.name or company.com
> e.g.: http://www.ford.com
> http://www.wegmans.com

Some search engines now have the u: search feature.
For example, searching u:ingram will take you to Ingram Micros home page without you having to know the URL or uniform resource locator (http://address).

RESOURCES to CONSULT FOR SEARCHING THE INTERNET EFFECTIVELY

Periodical Articles:

Courtois, Martin, William M. Baer, and Marcella Stark. "Cool tools for searching the web: a performance evaluation." *Online* November/December 1995 : 15-32.

Randall, Neil. "The search engine that could." *PC Magazine* September 1995 : 165+.

Scoville, Richard. "Find it on the net." *PC World* January 1996 : 125-130.

Webster, Kathleen and Kathryn Paul. "Beyond surfing:tools and techniques for searching the Web." *Feliciter* January 1996 : 48-54.

Web sites:

Help screens/instructions for Alta Vista, excite Netsearch, Lycos, WebCrawler

http://www.stark.k12.oh.us/Docs/search/
>   Judy Birmingham's excellent comparison in table form of various search engines.

http://www.indiana.edu/~librcsd/search/
>   Jian Liu's detailed look at search engines.

http://lcweb.loc.gov/global/internet/training.html
>   Library of Congress list of tutorials to learn and surf the 'Net.

http://www.library.nwu.edu/resources/internet/search/#top
>   Northwestern University's Internet resources

http://www.hamline.edu/library/bush/handouts/comparisons.html
>   Understanding and comparing Web search tools including a comparative study by Ian Winship.

http://www.ipl.org/classroom/userdocs/internet/engines.html
>   Compares several search engines including Alta Vista, Excite, Infoseek, Lycos, and Magellan.

http://info.anu.edu.au/courses/intro/wkbk/loc.html
http://info.anu.edu.au/courses/intro/wkbk/bg.html
>   Provides common search strategies.

http://info.anu.edu.au/elisa/elibrary/indexes1.html
>   Provides indexes and directories.

http://www.nlc-bnc.ca/publications/netnotes/notes15.htm
>   Useful article about search engines by David Jakob.

Workshop III. Evaluating and Citing Information Found on the Internet

Instructional material for Workshop III was partially based on Hope Tillman's presentation at Harvard University on "Evaluating Quality on the 'Net." (September 6, 1995). Other resources were consulted as well. (See list of resources consulted.)

The goals of Workshop III are that faculty at NCCC are able to evaluate information found on the Internet and that they are able to cite information found on the Internet.

Objectives of the Instruction:

Upon completion of this instruction session:
- Faculty are able to evaluate information found on the Internet for authoritativeness, timeliness, credibility, and reliability.
- Faculty are able cite information found on the Internet in *APA* and *MLA* formats.

Components of the Instruction:

Introduction and Overview: (10 minutes)

The librarian explains the goals and objectives of Workshop III. Faculty are asked to share their Internet searching experiences and knowledge of evaluating information.

Kind of Information Found on the 'Net: (30 minutes)

Kinds of information found on the Internet are presented. This includes self-published information, fugitive literature, association information, research project updates, advertising, and activist publishing. Examples of "bad" and "good" web sites are illustrated.

Evaluating Internet Information: (30 minutes)

Key questions to answer when evaluating information found on the Internet are covered. (See handout of questions appended that you may reproduce.) Faculty are encouraged to use this handout with their students. The librarian surfs the 'Net and asks faculty to evaluate sites found.

Citing Information Found on the Internet: (10 minutes)

How to cite information in *APA* and *MLA* formats is presented. Both handouts, "Citing Computerized/Electronic Sources in APA Style" and "Citing Computerized/Electronic Sources in MLA Style," are included for you to reproduce.

Conclusion: (10 minutes)

The librarian reviews the session and asks faculty if there are any further questions.

For more information, please see "Sources Consulted for Evaluating Information on the Internet."

Faculty Response:

Faculty response to the Teaching and Learning with Technology Series has been very positive. Learning to search the Internet effectively for information in a small group setting, having time to explore the Internet while being able to ask questions, and understanding how to evaluate the information found were mentioned by faculty to meet their needs. Most faculty expressed excitement over now being able to integrate the Internet at a basic level in their disciplines and confidence in being able to respond to student queries regarding the information superhighway.

EVALUATING INFORMATION FOUND ON THE INTERNET

Are the facts (information) presented accurately?
>Are they documented?
>Do they appear well-researched?

Are the facts (information) current for your topic?

Who is the audience?

Is the information biased?
>What is the purpose of the Web site?

Who are the authors or authority?
>What are their credentials?
>What is their educational background?
>Have they published?
>What is their experience in the field?
>Are they cited by others?
>What is their institutional affiliation?

What is the criteria for including the information?

What is the scope (coverage) of the site?
>What does it include as well as what does it exclude?
>If links are provided in the site, how are they evaluated for inclusion?

How does the information compare with other sources available on your topic?
>Both in print and electronic form? (Check with a librarian.)

Is the information/site stable?
>Will you be able to access the information again and again?

When was the information updated?

What information was updated?

SOURCES CONSULTED FOR EVALUATING INFORMATION ON THE INTERNET

Ciolek, T. Matthew. "Information Quality." World Wide Web Virtual Library.
http://coombs.anu.edu.au/WWWVL-InfoQuality.html
Site called "Information Quality" is edited by Dr. T. Matthew Ciolek. Includes definitions of information quality, ethics and etiquette, and citing electronic sources.

Grassian, Esther. "Thinking Critically about World Wide Web Resources."
http://www.library.ucla.edu/libraries/college/instruct/critical.htm
Grassian illuminates some valuable tips on evaluating information found on the Web.

Hincliffe, Lisa Janicke. "Resource Selection and Information Evaluation."
http://alexia.lis.uiuc.edu/~janicke/Evaluate.html
Discusses where information is found on the 'Net, and the accuracy and reliability of information. Compares evaluation methods of print and electronic (Internet) sources.

Ormondroyd, Joan, Michael Engle, and Tony Cosgrave. "How to Critically Analyze Information Sources
http://www.library.cornell.edu/okuref/research/skill26.htm
Information on evaluating information can be applied not only to print sources but electronic sources as well.

Tate, Marsha and Jan Alexander. "Teaching Critical Evaluation Skills for World Wide Web Resources." *Computers in Libraries* November/December 1996 : 49-55. See also web site at: http://www.widener.edu/widener.html

Tillman, Hope. "Evaluating Quality on the Net."
http://www.tiac.net/users/hope/findqual.html
Excellent site containing current information on evaluation. Information is from Hope Tillman's presentation "Evaluating the Quality of Information on the Internet or Finding a Needle in a Haystack" presented at the John F. Kennedy School of Government, Harvard University, September 6, 1995.

Evaluating Internet Information

Please complete this Worksheet

1.   What search engine did you use? (Circle one)

      Alta Vista   http://altavista.digital.com
      HOTBOT   http://www.hotabot.com
      Lycos   http://www.lycos.com
      Yahoo   http://www.yahoo.com
      Webcrawler   http://webcrawler.com

2.   What subject(s) did you type in for your search?

      _____

      _____

3.   How may "records" or "hits" did you retrieve?

      _____

4.   Click on one web site and go to it.
      What is the web address?

      http://...

5.   What is the name of the web site?

      _____

6.   What is the purpose of the web site?

      _____

      _____

      _____

7.   What kind of information is included in the web site?
      (Check all that apply.)

      _____ Advertising

      _____ Articles

      _____ Graphics (pictures)

      _____ Maps

      _____ Statistics

      _____ Other information:_____

      _____

8.   Who are the author(s) of the web site?

      _____

9.   What are the author(s) credentials?

      _____

10.   With what organization or institution are the authors affiliated? (college,
      university etc.)

      _____

11.   When was the web site last updated?

      _____

12.   How would this information be useful to you?
      If the information is not useful, why not?

      _____

      _____

      _____

Gail M. Staines, Ph.D. Coordinator of Library Instruction, Niagara County Community College © 1997

Citing Computerized/Electronic Sources in *APA* Style

Examples used in this handout follow the guidelines listed in the 4th edition of the *Publication Manual of the American Psychological Association.* For more examples see Xia Li and Nancy Crane. *Electronic Style: A Guide to Citing Electronic Information.* Westport, CT : Mecklermedia, 1966 or visit Janice R. Walker's site "APA-Style Citations of Electronic Sources" at http://www.cas.usf.edu/english/walker/apa.html

Citing Abstracts:

Author. (date). Article title. [Publication medium.] *Title of journal,* volume number, pages. Abstract from: Source retrieval number (if available).

O'Connor, B.P. & Molly, K. (1991). A test of the intellectual cycle of the popular biorhythm theory. [CD-ROM]. *The Journal of Psychology*, 125, 291-299. Abstract from: PsychLIT Item: 91-12568.

Citing Reference Sources on CD-ROM

Author. (date). Title of article. In *Reference source title* (version if given) [publication medium]. Place of publication : Producer or distributor.

Ashton, P.T. (1993) Psychology. In *New Grolier Multimedia Encyclopedia* (Release 6) [CD-ROM]. Danbury, CT : Grolier Inc.

Citing Electronic Mail Communications

Citing electronic mail communications is not recommended by *APA*. If e-mail communication has "scholarly relevance" include the citation in the text of your paper only. Do not cite it in the reference section of your paper.

In-text Citation:
(K.G. Johnson, personal communication, August 17, 1997)

Citing a Web Site

Author (if given). (date). Title of Article. *Title of complete work.* URL address (date visited).

(1997). "Should we be cloning around?" *Sci-Tech Story Page (CNN Interactive).* http://www.cnn.com/TECH/9702/24/cloned.sheep/index.html (11 March 1997).

Citing Computerized/Electronic Sources in *MLA* Style

Citing Abstracts

Author (if available). "Article title." *Journal title* Journal date : page(s). *computer database.* Publication medium. Producer or distributor. Data of database.

McGrath, Charles. "Mulligan Stew (golf tips for Bill Clinton)." *The New Yorker* 19 Sept. 1994: 116. *Infotrac Academic Index.* CD-ROM. Information Access. June 1995.

"Helping Consumers Avoid Sour Grapes." *USA Today* (magazine) August 1992 : 6+. *Infotrac Academic Index* CD-ROM. Information Access. June 1955.

Citing Reference Sources on CD-ROM

Author (if given). "Title of article." *Title of Reference Source.* Edition (if known). Release or version number (if given). CD-ROM. City of publisher : Publisher, Year.

Ashton, Patricia Teague. "Psychology." *New Grolier Multimedia Encyclopedia.* Rel. 6. CD-ROM. Danbury, CT : Grolier, Inc., 1993.

Citing Electronic Mail Communications

E-mail you receive:
Name of person writing e-mail. "Subject." E-mail to the author. Date.

Virtual, R.E. "Thank you for your letter." E-mail to the author. 22 September 1995.

E-mail between two people:
Name of person writing e-mail. "Subject." E-mail to name of person receiving e-mail. Date.

Raish, Martin. "Library Instruction on BI-L." E-mail to Nancy Warren. 12 August 1996.

E-mail Posted on a List:
Name of person posting message. "Subject." Date written. Online posting. Newsgroup name. Network name. Date.

Peterson, Linda. "Will Ross make a come back?" 7 July 1995. Online posting. Newsgroup   alt.politics.perot. Usenet. 21 July 1995.

Citing Information from a Computer Service:

Author (if given). "Article title." *Journal title* Journal date : page(s). *Database title.* Publication medium. Computer service name. Date accessed.

Stempen, Dave. "Natalie Merchant and the 10,000 Maniacs." *New York Times* 14 Feb. 1994, Late Ed : C3. *New York Times Online.* Online. Nexis. 20 March 1994.

Citing Information from Electronic Journals:

Author (if given). "Article title." *Journal title* Volume or issue number (Publication date) : Pages Publication medium. Computer network name. Date of access. Availability (if given).

Gillis, Stacy. "Mainstreaming through sympathy."
MYSTERIOUS BYTES 3 (March 1997) : n.pag.
Online. Internet. 15 April 1977.
Available: http://www/db.dk/dbaa/jbs/mb/mb3.htm#link5

Citing a Web Site:

Author (if given). "Title of article or work." *Title of complete work.* URL address (date visited).

"Should we be cloning around?" *Sci-Tech Story Page (CNN Interactive).*
http://www.cnn.com/TECH9702/24/cloned.sheep/index.html (11 March 1997)

For more information and other examples, please see *MLA Handbook for Writers of Research Papers* by Joseph Gibaldi, 4th ed. (1995) and Xia Li and Nancy Crane, *Electronic Style: A Guide to Citing Electronic Information.* Westport, CT : Mecklermedia, 1996 or visit Janice R. Walker's site "MLA-Style Citations of Electronic Sources" at http://www.cas.usf.edu/english/walker/mla.html

World Wide Web Navigation; Teaching Small Groups in 50 Minutes Using Hands-on Exercises

TEXAS A&M LIBRARIES WEB INSTRUCTION TEAM

J.L. Hart, E. Gass, S.K. Sandall, D.Y. Xiao, A.P. Daily
TEXAS A&M UNIVERSITY

Circumstances for the Instruction Session:

This course was collaboratively developed by a team of five librarians from Sterling C. Evans Library and the West Campus Library (business, agriculture and life sciences) at Texas A&M University, College Station. The idea for the course grew out of the perception that instruction focusing on the content of the World Wide Web (WWW) coupled with the concepts of database searching was needed and was not available elsewhere on campus. With many databases migrating to the Web, and more and more class assignments requiring Web searching, this class fills a growing need.

The goal of the class is to teach students the search process, and how to locate, evaluate, collect, save, and cite information found on the WWW. The sessions are designed for undergraduate or graduate students, faculty, and staff who are novices in searching the World Wide Web.

The length of the session is 50 minutes, which corresponds with the university class schedule. Sessions are scheduled to be equally available to students with MWF or TTh class schedules, and are offered every semester at each library.

The class, taught by a team of librarians, provides hands-on experience for each participant. Teacher to participant ratio is purposely kept low to provide individualized assistance with the exercises. Class size is limited to the number of available computer workstations. Ideally this means one participant per computer, or at most two to a computer, in which case the participants take turns at the keyboard.

Objectives of the Instruction:

- To learn the basic features and navigational tools of the Netscape browser,
- To become aware of the number and variety of available search engines and subject directories,
- To learn to execute basic searches with selected WWW search engines,
- To understand the transferable skills involved in electronic searching,
- To learn to critically evaluate sites, and
- To learn to collect and organize useful sites with the bookmark feature.

Components of the Library Instruction:

PREPARATION:

Flexibility of the instructor is the first key in preparing a successful course on searching the WWW. Since the Web is a dynamic resource that constantly changes, updating the course outline, the PowerPoint presentation, and the handouts and exercises is a regular, expected occurrence.

The class is advertised through a variety of media. Posters are placed in the library lobbies with quarter-page size leaflets that can be taken as a reminder of the class times. Flyers are distributed around campus by student workers. The class is advertised in the student newspaper, on a faculty and staff campus-wide listserv, on the libraries' Web pages, and on table tents (small, folded placards) placed in student dining areas.

Class participants are asked to sign-in and pick up handouts when they arrive. The sign-in sheet includes columns for name, university status, major department, whether or not they are new to the university, and how they learned about the instruction session (useful for future publicity). Participants with similar subject disciplines can be paired together for the hands-on component if necessary.

CLASSROOM PRESENTATION (25 minutes)

After the instructors introduce themselves and the handouts are reviewed, the PowerPoint presentation begins. PowerPoint is presentation software which allows the user to make a "slide show" that can be saved to a disk. The instructor toggles back and forth between the PowerPoint presentation and Netscape to demonstrate Netscape features and search services as necessary. Highlights of the presentation include explanations and/or demonstrations of:

- The Internet and its basic tools (e-mail, telnet, FTP, USENET, gopher, WWW).

- The basic components of a Web page (URL, hypertext links) and navigational features of the Netscape browser. Explain why a Web browser is currently the most effective way to explore the Internet.

- A framework for finding information on the Web by thinking of search services in terms of subject directories and search engines. *This will evolve as search services continue to integrate subject directories of Web sites with Internet search engines.*

- Skills needed for developing effective searches. Explain Boolean logic, proximity operators, and truncation, and stress that these are transferable skills used in search strategy for electronic resources.

- Yahoo and Alta Vista. Use the sites' help screens to explain search tips for the services. Enter the searches with proper syntax for the search services, but do not execute them unless time allows.

- The bookmark feature of Netscape to collect useful sites. Discuss the value of saving bookmarks to a disk and importing the collection onto other computers with an Internet connection. *Saving bookmarks to a disk is an exercise for the class and one of the handouts includes directions for saving, downloading, and uploading bookmarks.*

- Criteria for evaluating and citing Internet information is emphasized. Refer participants to the handouts that provide a list of WWW evaluation points and a URL for MLA Internet citation information.

    Note: The following are included with this chapter:
    - Text used in the PowerPoint presentation
    - Yahoo and Alta Vista search options
    - Hands-on exercise
    - Handouts:
        Developing an Effective Search Strategy for the WWW
        Netscape Bookmark Collection
        WWW Evaluation Checklist
        Web Links to Citing Internet Sources
    - Bibliography of WWW sites related to Web instruction

Hands-on Exercise (25 minutes)

A different instructor takes over the class at this point and facilitates the exercise (see handout). The other instructors in the classroom rove the area to assist with any questions and concerns. Instructors can assist participants in applying evaluation criteria to sites they view together.

The nature of the exercise allows for practice of general search and retrieval skills on topics of interest to the participants. The exercise begins with accessing the library's Web page, which has links to subscription databases and catalogs via the Internet.

Next, participants practice keyword selection and search strategy development by locating Web sites in a subject area of interest to them. Sites are bookmarked, exported, and imported to practice Netscape's features for collection. Finally, the evaluation exercise gives experience in typing mixed case URLs, using forms, and interacting with a site.

Evaluation:

Participants' Evaluation
To elicit opinion about the library instruction session, and to have fun practicing, the participants are asked to send an e-mail postcard commenting about the session to one instructor via the "Electric Postcard" website at MIT http://postcards.www.media.mit.edu/Postcards. Comments received have emphasized the value of the hands-on component and the guided practice.

Instructors' Evaluation
The class must be updated continually because search services and Web sites constantly change. The instructors meet periodically to evaluate the last round of sessions, and each instructor has a predetermined responsibility for the currency of a portion of the class. In addition, organization of material and teaching methods are also reviewed and adapted.

Variations:

1. A flip chart or an overhead projector with transparencies may be used instead of PowerPoint slides.

2. Students may sit at workstations for the entire class, or sit classroom-style for the presentation and move to workstations for the hands-on portion of the session.

3. Trained Web-knowledgeable student workers can act as assistants for the hands-on portion if other librarians are not available.

4. Participants can turn in a one-page paper with their search strategy and an evaluation of a Web site if the instructor wants to be able to provide feedback on the skills learned.

Suggested text for visuals;
slides, transparencies, or flip chart

1. Introduction

Using the World Wide Web for Research

[name of your institution]

2. Topics

- What is the Internet?
- World Wide Web and Netscape
- Finding Information on the WWW
- Organizing information from the WWW
- Evaluating and Citing Electronic Information

3. What is the Internet?

- Worldwide network of computer networks
- Computers communicate using TCP/IP
- Major tools include e-mail, telnet, file transfer protocol (FTP), USENET, gopher, and World Wide Web (WWW)
  Dynamic! Constantly Changing!

4. Netscape: A World Wide Web Browser

- The **WWW** is a hypertext-based system for finding and accessing Internet resources
- Integrates Internet tools
- A Web Browser is the most effective way to explore the Internet

5. Finding Information on the Web

- Various types of data are available:
    text, graphics, sound,
    chart, video, etc.
- To search for data, a search service is used:
    Subject Directories:
        Yahoo, Galaxy, Magellan, etc.
    Search engines:
        Alta Vista, HotBot, Lycos, Infoseek, etc.

6. Developing Search Strategies

- Think of some "key words" to describe your topic
- Read information provided with the search engine to engage in the most effective search
- If possible, combine your terms to find the most relevant information.

7. Organizing WWW Information

- Collect your favorite sites by creating a list of bookmarks
- Organize your bookmarks into folders
- Save your bookmarks to a disk
- Create a Web page for your bookmarks

8. Criteria for Evaluating Internet Information

- Accuracy
- Authority
- Coverage
- Currency
- Objectivity

9. Tips for Citing Web Information

- Remember the goal of a citation is to allow the reader to retrieve the item
- Consider printing a copy of the item, or mailing it to yourself via e-mail
- Punctuate and capitalize the URL of the source exactly as it appears in the Location box

Sample Searches in YAHOO!

1.   **Q: Are there any resources pertaining to acid rain on the WWW?**

     If just going through the **subject headings** versus searching on the first screen, this is the order:
     Society and Culture:Environment and Nature: Pollution: Acid Rain;
     select "EcoNet Acid Rain Resources."

     Keyword Search: acid rain
     Under the "Yahoo Site" listings—select "EcoNet Acid Rain Resources."

2.   **Q: What current research is being done on the herbicide 2,4-D, if any?**

     If just going through the **subject headings** versus searching on the first screen, this is the order:
     Science:Agriculture:Weed Control;
     select "2,4-D Herbicide Research Data."

     Keyword Search: 24d or 2, 4-D
     Under the "Yahoo Site" listings—select "2,4-D Herbicide Research Data."

3.   **Q: Who are all the State Senators for Texas and their mailing addresses?**

     If just going through the **subject headings** versus searching on the first screen, this is the order:
     Regional:U.S. States:Texas:Government:Elected Officials: State Senators;
     select "Yahoo Site" listings "Texas Senate Members."

     Keyword Search: elected officials texas
     Under the "Yahoo Site" listings—select "Texas Senate Members."

4.   **Q: Where can I find the most current NASDAQ prices, indexes, and volume changes for NASDAQ itself as well as for individual companies?**

     If just going through the **subject headings** versus searching on the first screen, this is the order:
     Business and Economy:Markets and investments:Exchanges:Stock Exchanges:NASDAQ;
     select "Nasdaq FullQuote."

     Keyword Search: NASDAQ
     Under the "Yahoo Site" listings—select "Nasdaq FullQuote."

Sample Searches in ALTA VISTA

1. **Q: How are genetically engineered food plants regulated?**

    Simple Keyword Search: +regulation +"genetically engineered food plants"

    Select "Regulation of Genetically Engineered Organisms and Products."

2. **Q: What current research is being done on the herbicide 2,4-D, if any?**

    Simple Keyword Search: +2,4-D and +research

    Select "2,4-Dichlorophenoxyacetic Acid (2,4-D)."

3. **Q: What are the most current trade statistics for the United States?**

    Simple Keyword Search: +"United States" +"trade statistics"

    Select "Trade Statistics."

4. **Q: What is available on minority businesses in Houston?**

    Simple Keyword Search: +"minority business*" and +Houston

    Select "Houston Minority Business Council Home Page."

Using the World Wide Web for Research

Select a topic of particular interest to you and use it to complete steps 3–5 of this exercise. You should use general search and retrieval skills that have been discussed and demonstrated in class.

Topic...

Step 1 From **TAMU** homepage, click on Libraries/Reference
Go to the Evans Library **Catalogs and Databases** page
Add bookmark
Go back to TAMU homepage

Step 2 Go to**Yahoo**
Add bookmark

Step 3 Search Yahoo
Pick a topic of your choice
Narrow your search
Add bookmarks for sites of interest
Go back to TAMU home page

Step 4 Go to **Alta Vista**
Add bookmark

Step 5 Search Alta Vista
Pick a topic of your choice
Narrow your search
Add bookmarks for sites of interest

Step 6 **Export bookmarks** to a disk

Step 7 **View bookmarks** as a Web page

Step 8 Go to **The Electric Postcard** homepage.
http://postcards.www.media.mit.edu/Postcards
We want your input. Please send a postcard and tell us the most important thing you learned from this class. Send the postcard to jlhart@tamu.edu
Thanks!

Developing an Effective Search Strategy

for the World Wide Web

1. **Think about what you want to research** and develop a list of important **key words** and **concepts** to describe your topic. Include **synonyms** of your key words. You will probably have to play with various combinations of these words to retrieve a fair amount of appropriate information.

2. **Identify appropriate search services** to perform the search.

3. **Consult Online Help** to determine how to input your key words. You may be able to empower your search by using **Boolean Logic, Proximity Operators,** and **Truncation.**

➤   **Boolean Logic**—combine terms using the words "and," "or" and "not" to narrow or broaden the search and focus what is returned by the computer. Forms of operators may vary between search services.

   recycle **AND** plastic [narrows the focus]
   recycle **OR** reuse [broadens the focus]
   recycle **NOT** glass [narrows the focus]

➤   **Proximity Operators**—specify how close two or more words will be in the documents that are retrieved. The operators often used are "near," "with," and "adjacent." Some search services use quotation marks to indicate a phrase, e.g. "recycling center."

➤   **Truncation**—cut a key word to its root and add a truncation symbol to retrieve all the variations of the word. Truncation symbols vary so be sure to read the text with the search service to determine what to use.

   recycl* [retrieves the words recycle, recycles, recycling, recyclable, etc]

4. **Be aware** that some databases you can access through the WWW incorporate controlled or standardized language (**subject descriptors**) in their systems. Just because you describe something a certain way does not mean the database does, *e.g., " Native Americans"* are officially described as *"Indians of North America"* by libraries which follow the Library of Congress classification system. If possible, look at a record you've retrieved by using a key word search and identify the subject descriptors to perform a more comprehensive subject search.

5. Always **Read All The Screen (RATS!)** to find out how to use the search service or database. Commands for getting into **Online Help** should be visible.

NETSCAPE BOOKMARK COLLECTION

- To collect bookmarks:
    Select **Bookmarks/Add Bookmark** when you want to remember a site, <u>or</u>
    Select **Window/History,** click on the URL you want to bookmark, then select Create Bookmark.

- To organize bookmarks in folders:
    Set up categories such as Internet Search Tools, E-journals, Biology, etc.
    Select **Bookmarks/Go to Bookmarks** then select **Item/Insert Folder**
    Enter the name of the new header in the Name field; click **OK**
    Drag and drop items onto the folder category.

- To export (save) bookmarks to a disk:
    Insert a disk in the "**a**" drive
    Select **Bookmarks/Go to Bookmarks**
    Select **File Menu/Save As**...
    Name your file (bookmark.htm)
    Select the **a** drive to save.

- To import bookmarks:
    Insert a disk in "**a**" drive
    Select **Bookmarks/Go to Bookmarks**
    Select **File/Import**
    Select the "**a**" drive to import.

- To view your bookmarks as a Web page:
    Select **File/Open File**
    Open your bookmark file (bookmark.htm)
    Add your bookmark list as a bookmark.

INTERNET SITES TO ADD TO YOUR BOOKMARK COLLECTION

Internet
Internet Navigator (tutorial)
http://www.lib.utah.edu/navigator/discovery/discover.html

TAMU Databases and Catalogs
http://www.tamu.edu/library/catdata.html

Citations
Beyond the MLA Handbook:Documenting Electronic Sources on the Internet
by Andrew Harnack and Gene Keppinger
http://falcon.eku.edu/honors/beyond-mla

WWW Site Evaluation

Checklist

ACCURACY
- No typographical, grammatical, or spelling errors (leads to inaccurate information)
- Statistical data is clearly labeled and easy to read
- All sources of information are clearly stated and/or properly cited
- The information is presented in an orderly, logical or convenient manner
- Notice is given of the need for special software, hardware or multimedia viewers
- The page(s) are easy to load (not too many graphics or a slow modem on the host server)
- The page(s) can be properly viewed by all browsers

AUTHORITY
- The author's/sponsor's name is clearly given along with the qualifications
- The author's/sponsor's purpose/goals are clearly given
- Contact information is given for the page's author(s) and sponsor(s)
- Copyrights are clearly stated (owner (s) and date(s)) where applicable

COVERAGE
- It is clear as to whether the page has been completed, or is still under construction
- When there is a print equivalent to the Web page, it is clear whether the entire printed work is available on the web or only parts of it, as well as how other print and electronic resources compare to the web document (i.e. more current)
- The site is valuable as compared to other sources of information on the topic

CURRENCY
- Dates for the following are clearly indicated or can be easily determined:
- Date the page was written
- Date the page was first placed on the Web
- Date the page was last revised
- Collection date is given for statistical data
- The edition number of a printed work from which information has been taken is clearly stated/labeled

OBJECTIVITY
- The information is intended as a public service as opposed to an advertisement
- When advertising is present it is clearly delineated from the informational content
- There are few to no biases in the document/site (i.e., limited coverage, point(s) of view)

Citation Styles for WWW Sites—Help Sheet

General

    Classroom Connect: How to Cite Internet Addresses
        http://www.classroom.net/classroom/CitingNetResources.html

    Electronic Style Page
        http://funnelweb.utcc.utk.edu/~hoemann/whats.html

    Guide for Citing electronic Information
        http://www.wilpaterson.edu/wpcpages/library/citing.htm

    ISO (International Organization for Standardization)
        http://www.nlc-bnc.ca/iso/tc46sc9/standard/690-2e.htm

APA (American Psychological Association)

    APA Style Electronic Formats
        http://www.westwords.com/guffey/apa.html

    ASCII Citation of Electronic Documents
        http://library.ccsu.ctstateu.edu/~history/docs/cite.html

    Electronic Sources: APA Style of Citation
        http://www.uvm.edu/~xli/reference/apa.html

    Walker/ACW Style Sheet
        http://www.cas.usf.edu/english/walker/apa.html

    Web Extension to American Psychological Association Style (WEAPAS)
        http://www.beadsland.com/weapas/

Chicago Manual of Style

    Chicago Style Citation of Computer documents
        http://library.ccsu.ctstateu.edu/~history/docs/chicago.html

    Electronic Sources Style Guide: Citation Components and Examples
        http://libits.library.ualberta.ca/library_html/help/pathfinders/style/stylecp.html

MLA (Modern Language Association)

    Beyond the MLA Handbook: Documenting Electronic Sources on the Internet
        http://falcon.eku.edu/honors/beyond-mla/

    Citing Electronic Materials with the New MLA Guidelines
        http://www-dept.usm.edu/~engdept/mla/rules.html

    Electronic Sources: MLA Style of Citation
        http://www.uvm.edu/~xli/reference/mla.html

    MLA Electronic Citation: Citing Online Sources (Internet and Westlaw)
        http://www.nhmccd.cc.tc/kc/mla-internet.html

    MLA-Style Citations of Electronic Sources (Endorsed by the Alliance for Computers & Writing)
        http://www.cas.usf.edu/english/walker/mla.html

Subject Specific Style Guidelines

Below are the various subject areas that have acceptable formats for citing electronic resources available on the Web. The bold in parentheses is the citation style after which that site has modeled its examples.

Government Information

Guide to Citing Government Information Sources (*MLA*; **Garner, 1993**)
http://unr.edu/homepage/duncan/cite.html
Uncle Sam—Brief Guide to Citing Government Publications (**Garner and Smith, 1984**)
http://www.lib.memphis.edu/gpo/citeweb.htm

History

A Brief Citation Guide for Internet Sources in History and the Humanities (**Turabian**)
http://h-et2.msu.edu/~africa/citation.html
Mirror site:
http://www.nmmc.com/libweb/employee/citguide.htm
Citing Electronic Information in History Papers (**Turabian**)
http://www.people.memphis.edu/~mcrouse/elcite.html

Humanities

A Brief Citation Guide for Internet Sources in History and the Humanities (**Turabian**)
http://h-net2.msu.edu/~africa/citation.html
Mirror site:
http://www.nmmc.com/libweb/employee/citguide.htm
Electronic Style Page (**Chicago; MLA**)
http://funnelweb.utcc.utk.edu/~hoemann/disciplines.html

Medicine

Electronic Style Page (**Patrias, 1991**)
http://funnelweb.utcc.utk.edu/~hoemann/disciplines.html
Guidelines for Referencing GDB (Human Genome Project)
http://gdbwww.gdb.org/gdb/gdb-ref.html

Sciences

Scientific Citation for Electronic Sources (**Council of Biology Editors (CBE)**)
http://library.morningside.edu/scistyle.htm

Social Sciences

Electronic Style Page (**APA**)
http://funnelweb.utcc.utk.edu/~hoemann/disciplines.html

Bibliography of WWW Sites Related to Web Instruction

Contents:
History of the Internet
Background Information
Searching Techniques
Search Engines; Evaluations, Matrices, and Lists
Guides and Tutorials on the Internet and about the Internet
Evaluation of Web Sites

History of the Internet

Title: Internet Timeline
URL: ftp://access.tucson.org/pub/internet/timeline.txt

Title: Welcome to Life on the Internet
URL: http://www.pbs.org/internet/

Title: Origins of the Internet (Editor's Notes: Ring That Bell . . .)
URL: http://www.boardwatch.com/mag/95/jun/bwm1.htm

Title: Internet Background and Basics
URL: http://www.tectrix.com/links/internet.html
    ('History of the Internet'; Internet Timeline by BBN)

Title: Short History of the Internet
URL: http://www.forthnet.gr/forthnet/isoc/short.history.of.internet

Background Information

Title: Internet Background and Basics
URL: http://www.tectrix.com/links/internet.html

Title: Internet Help
URL: http://www.albany.edu/library/internet/
    (A Basic Guide to the Internet)

Title: The Matrix of Internet Catalogs and Search Engines: Administrative Documents
URL: http://www.ambrosiasw.com/~fprefect/matrix/matrix.html
    (Vocabulary Page)

Title: Netskills Searching Resource Pages
URL: http://www.netskills.ac.uk/resources/searching/
    (Netskills Glossary)

Searching Techniques

Title: Internet Help
URL: http://www.albany.edu/library/internet/

Title: A Higher Signal - To - Noise Ratio: Effective Use of Web Search Engines
URL: http://www.state.wi.us/agencies/dpi/www/search.html

Title: Sink or Swim: Internet Search Tools & Techniques
URL: http://oksw01.okanagan.bc.ca/libr/connect96/search.htm

Title: Netskills Searching Resource Pages
URL: http://www.netskills.ac.uk/resources/searching/

Title: CNET Features - Digital Life - Can You Trust Your Search Engine?
URL: http://www.cnet.com/content/Features/Dlife/Search/

Title: The Matrix - Of Internet Catalogs and Search Engines
URL: http://www.ambrosiasw.com/~fprefect/matrix/matrix.html
      (Some Hard Answers)

Title: Web Search Engines: A Webliography/Bibliography
URL: http://www.state.wi.us/agencies/dpi/www/srch_bib.html

Guides and Tutorials on the Internet and about the Internet

Title: CIS178 - Lessons
URL: http://www.capital.pcc.edu/courses/cis178/lessons.html
    (Week 5 - Accessing Information, and
    Week 6 - Organizing/Evaluating Search Results)

Title: Internet Navigator Course Introduction
URL: http://medstat.med.utah.edu/navigator/intro/intro.html

Title: Netscape Tutorial
URL: http://w3.ag.uiuc.edu/AIM/Discovery/Net/www/netscape/index.html

Title: The Roadmap96 Workshop Syllabus
URL: http://ua1vm.ua.edu/~crispen/syllabus.html

Title: Zen and the Art of the Internet - Table of Contents
URL: http://access.tucson.org/zen/zen-1.0_toc.html

Title: InterNIC 15 Minute Series
URL: http://rs.internic.net/nic-support/15min/

Title: Panhandle Pages - Beginners Central (Intro)
URL: http://www.digital-cafe.com/~webmaster/begin00.html

Title: Entering the World-Wide Web: A Guide to Cyberspace
URL: http://www.hcc.hawaii.edu/guide/www.guide.html

Title: Learn the Net
URL: http://www.learnthenet.com/

Title: Netscape 1.2 Tutorial
URL: http://www.netstrider.com/tutorials/netscape/1.2/

Title: Netscape 2.0 Bookmarks Tutorial for Windows 3.1
URL: http://library.berkeley.edu:8000/NS/bkmk/win31/contents.html

Evaluation of Web Sites

Title: Assessing Quality and Value of Internet Resources
URL: http://www.fiu.edu/~clementg/medical/slaqv.html

Title: Teaching Critical Evaluation Skills for World Wide Web Resources
URL: http://www.science.widener.edu/~withers/webeval.htm

Title: Beyond Cool - Analog Models for Reviewing Digital Resources
URL: http://www.onlineinc.com/online/online/onlinemag/SeptOL/rettig9.html

Title: Evaluating Internet Information
URL: http://milton.mse.jhu.edu:8001/research/education/net.html

Title: Thinking Critically about World Wide Web Resources
URL: http://www.library.ucla.edu/libraries/college/instruct/critical.htm

Title: Evaluating World Wide Web Information
URL:
http://thorplus.lib.purdue.edu/research/classes/gs175/3gs175/evaluation.html

Title: How to Critically Analyze Information Sources
URL: http://urisref.library.cornell.edu/skill26.htm

Title: Internet Help
URL: http://www.albany.edu/library/internet/
    (Evaluating Internet Resources)

"Searching the Net:" Using Web-Based Lessons to Teach Internet Searching

John J. Burke

Electronic Resources Librarian

FAIRMONT STATE COLLEGE, FAIRMONT, WV

Introduction

Many libraries face the task of providing instruction to those wishing to use the Internet to find information. "Searching the Net," the session introduced below, not only demonstrates one way to meet this goal, it also utilizes the Internet as the medium for instruction. With access to a World Wide Web server and a growing knowledge of Hypertext Markup Language (HTML), any library can teach nearly anything to anyone with access to the Internet. "Searching the Net" can be used as is or can serve as a model to create other online instructions.

Circumstances for the Instruction:

This session was created to give interested individuals an opportunity to learn how to search the Internet for information. It was designed to be used by anyone with access to the Internet and a World Wide Web browser. I announced it to the Fairmont State College community through a print handout mailed to faculty members and through postings sent to FSCNET-L, the campus Internet users' discussion group that I manage. Faculty and staff make up the majority of Internet users at FSC, with most student use limited to specific class assignments.

The discussion group audience includes users not affiliated with nor connected to the campus, so I hoped to reach users other than faculty and staff and located beyond the environs of the college. While originally intended as a test of Internet instruction, the session will reside online as an ongoing point of instruction.

Objectives of the Instruction:

The session was designed to teach participants the following:
- what types of information exist on the Internet
- how to define and refine searches
- how to identify common Internet search engines and reference collections
- how to form strategies for seeking information from these sources
- how to evaluate the sources they find and how to cite them in formal written or electronic work

Components of the Instruction:

"Searching the Net" consists of an introduction Web page, five separate lessons that explore various aspects of searching for Internet resources, and an assignment to test the effectiveness of the lessons. Users start from the introduction page and choose from the lessons, which are then linked both to the next lesson in sequence and to the introduction page. The lessons include textual information on their aspects along with links to Internet sites that assist in conveying the concepts discussed to users. Finally, users complete the assignment, which is then e-mailed to the session instructor for evaluation.

The lessons can all be viewed during one session or at an individual's convenience. This removes time as a limiting factor for the session. While standard instruction sessions are designed to have a set duration, "Searching the Net" can be accessed at the user's pace, at any time of day, and over the course of days or weeks. My offering of it was not limited to a certain deadline for completion (indeed, it is still ongoing), but such a limit could be set for more directed offerings.

As the introduction page of the session indicates, I coupled the "Searching the Net" lessons and assignment with discussion on FSCNET-L. This provided a forum for users to ask questions about the lessons or to make suggestions for improving them. If the session (or a similar one) was focused at a particular class, an electronic discussion group may not be necessary unless there are a large number of lessons or there are other points that the class instructor or session instructor wish to communicate. In this event, an e-mail address (preferably the session instructor's) should be provided to participants for the same purpose that the discussion group served.

The requirements for undertaking such a session are as follows:
1. an interested audience with Internet access,
2. HTML files containing the instructional material,
3. space on a Web server, and
4. the knowledge and/or technical support to put the previous three pieces together.

An effort of this sort might be requested by an individual instructor or could be an ongoing, multiple-use session. The preparation time required would make the latter preferable, but there may be an instance of a single distance education class that would require some type of library instruction. Once the lessons or other instructional material have been written, they must be tagged with HTML to make them readable by Web browsers (the software that allows one to view Web pages). I hope that my pages provide a model or foundation upon which you can build your HTML knowledge.

The server may be one managed within the library or perhaps elsewhere at the institution. Check with support personnel to see what procedures must be followed to place pages on the server. In the end, the session will be in place and ready for use by its intended audience with little required of the session instructor other than fielding questions.

Evaluation of the Session

The sole means for evaluating "Searching the Net" is the completion of the assignment. It includes four multi-part questions that directly test the user's ability:

- to form search statements,
- to identify key terms,
- to use Internet search engines, and
- to cite the sites found.

Following the questions is a blank space for general comments and blanks for users to fill in their names and e-mail addresses. Upon selection of the "Send" button, the answers, comments, and name and e-mail address are sent to the session instructor via e-mail as a form. A free mailer program is used to complete the delivery of the forms.

The assignment allows users to evaluate their skills independently and then send the results to the session instructor for feedback. In turn, the session and class instructors can compare the aggregate results of the users to see if the lessons were misleading or lacking in some areas. This aggregate can be used further by the session instructor to compare the results of the current class to those of earlier classes. Lessons and assignment questions can then be adapted as needed to better fit the instructional objectives.

Alternative Suggestions

This discussion and the HTML files in this chapter will enable a library to put "Searching the Net" in place as is or to adapt the session for local needs. Beyond this use, I offer it as a model for what libraries can do to teach a variety of skills in an online, self-directed tutorial manner. Although online instruction is ideally suited to teaching Internet concepts and resources, it can be utilized for subjects involving any types of material or resources: print, electronic, online, or any combination of these. To teach a session on musical resources in a particular library, for instance, one need not look at the Internet as anything more than a means of communicating the material. Do not feel called to add Internet sites gratuitously unless they fit into the lesson.

Anything that can be taught in a live session can be presented online. Text alone will work for many sessions. Depending on the computer capacities of the audience, a nearly unlimited array of graphical options is also available to session instructors. My personal goal for the future is to develop an online tutorial for using the OPAC at Fairmont State College, which will feature users jumping back and forth between the OPAC and the lesson. The mechanics for this are demonstrated in the "Searching the Net" assignment. I believe that the possibilities of this type of session are endless, and are essential to library instruction as libraries reach out to users who are geographically distant and pressed for time.

"Search the Net" Assignment

[The HTML which follows is the text of the Internet assignment discussed in this chapter .]

<HTML>
<body background="http://129.71.46.56/images/paper3.gif">
Searching the Net: Fall 1996<p>
<hr><p>
Graduation Assignment <p>
<p>
This assignment is a means for you to test your Net searching
abilities. Follow along with the questions, entering your
responses in the space provided. Once you have completed the
last question, choose "Send" to send the assignment to me for
grading. If you wish to reset the assignment and enter new
responses, choose "Clear".<p>
(Note: the assignment may not work with a graphical browser in
that your responses may not be saved if you leave this page to
look at an earlier lesson or to connect with Yahoo!. I am
looking for a fix for this).<p>
<FORM ACTION="http://www.cgi-free.com/mailer.cgi?jjb123"
METHOD=POST>
<ol>
<li>In the following topic sentence, what are the keywords or key
terms (as described in <a
href="http://129.71.46.56/seminar/stnless1.htm">Lesson #1</a>)?
List them in the space below the sentence.<p>
"I am looking for information on cooking fish."<p>
<INPUT NAME="1" SIZE=50><p><p>
<li>Now take those keywords and think about synonyms or alternate
terms that could be used (also described in Lesson #1). List
them below:<p>
<TEXTAREA NAME="2" ROWS=4 COLs=60></TEXTAREA><p><p>
<li>Now take the terms you listed above and perform a search in
Yahoo using what you feel is the best combination of them. After
completing your search, return to this page by using your "Back"
command. You may wish to look over the questions below before
you do your search. Connect to <a
href="http://yahoo.com">Yahoo!</a><p>
What did you enter on the search line in Yahoo!?<p>
<INPUT NAME="3a" SIZE=50> <p>
How many sites did Yahoo! find?<p>
<INPUT NAME="3b" SIZE=50><p>

Find a site that looks useful to you and write a citation for it
below, using the rules suggested in <a
href="http://129.71.46.56/seminar/stnless5.htm">Lesson #5.</a><p>
<TEXTAREA NAME="3c" ROWS=4 COLs=60></TEXTAREA><p><p>
<li>Now search for the topic in #1 in Alta Vista. After
completing your search, return to this page by using your "Back"
command. You may wish to look over the questions below before
you do your search. Connect to <a

href="http://altavista.digital.com">Alta Vista.</a><p>
What did you enter on the search line in Alta Vista?<p>
<INPUT NAME="4a" SIZE=50><p>
How many sites did Alta Vista find?<p>
<INPUT NAME="4b" SIZE=50><p>
Find a site that looks useful to you and write a citation for it
below, using the rules suggested in <a
href="http://129.71.46.56/seminar/stnless5.htm">Lesson #5.</a><p>
<TEXTAREA NAME="4c" ROWS=4 COLs=60></TEXTAREA><p><p></ol>
Your name: <INPUT NAME="name" SIZE=50><p>
Your e-mail address: <INPUT NAME="e-mail" SIZE=40><p>
Please enter any comments about the Searching the Internet
lessons below:<p>
<TEXTAREA NAME="comments" ROWS=4 COLs=60></TEXTAREA><p>
<TABLE COLSPEC="L20 L20" WIDTH=95%>
<TR><TD><CENTER><INPUT TYPE="submit" VALUE="SEND">
</center></TD><TD>
<CENTER><INPUT TYPE="reset" Value="CLEAR">
</center></TD></TR>
</TABLE><p>
</FORM>
Thanks for taking the graduation assignment! I will be sure to
reply to you and let you know how you did. <p>
Back to the <A HREF =
"http://129.71.46.56/seminar/stnintro.htm">Searching the
Internet</A> page <P>

<P ALIGN=Right><HR><A HREF=http://www.cgi-free.com/><IMG
ALIGN=Right
SRC=http://www.cgi-free.com/cgifree.gif ALT=CGI Free WIDTH=111
HEIGHT=31
BORDER=0 TARGET=_top></A><FONT SIZE=-1><B>CGI Free</B> is a great
service, all for free, where you may download CGI
Scripts, or
use them on <B>CGI Free's</B>
Server, for quick, and simple access.</FONT><HR>
</HTML>

<HTML>
<body background="http://129.71.46.56/images/paper3.gif">
<center>Fairmont State College Libraries</center>
<hr>
<center><h2>Searching the Net</h2></center><p>
Welcome to Searching the Net, the Ruth Ann Musick Library's
Internet Seminar for Fall
semester 1996! The seminar is comprised of five lessons which
will introduce you to
searching for information on the Internet. Once you have
completed reading the lessons
and trying out the exercises included, you will be ready to
search the Net effectively. <P>
<P>
The lessons appeared initially on October 25, 1996, and you are
invited to experience

them at your leisure. They are designed to be short and easy to read, and each includes
suggested sites to look at or sample searches to try. The lessons will remain in this
location for the forseeable future, so you can use them as reference materials for your Net
searching.<P>
<P>
The lessons are not written with any particular type of Internet account in mind. They can
be used from FSCVAX or FSCAXP accounts, as well as various WVNET accounts and
those of other Internet service providers. They concentrate on the World Wide Web for
the most part, requiring only a browser that can handle forms. This will work fine for
users at FSC and those with accounts from most other providers. If you have any account
specific questions, please let me or FSCNET-L know by sending an e-mail.<P>
<P>
Discussion and questions about the lessons and our topic will be entertained on FSCNET-
L, an electronic discussion group. It can be subscribed to by sending an e-mail message to
listserv@wvnvm.wvnet.edu without a subject, but with the command subscribe fscnet-l
yourfirstname yourlastname in the message body. You can send mail to all FSCNET-L
subscribers by sending your message to fscnet-l@wvnvm.wvnet.edu (and be sure to
include a subject). Discussion of the lessons will start around the same time that the
lessons appear and last until there is no longer interest in them.<P>
<P>
I hope you enjoy the lessons!<P>
<P>
John J. Burke <P>
<hr>
<ul>
<li><a href="http://129.71.46.56/seminar/stnless1.htm">Lesson 1:</a> What Are You Looking For? <p>
<li><a href="http://129.71.46.56/seminar/stnless2.htm">Lesson 2:</a> What Information Is Out There? <p>
<li><a href="http://129.71.46.56/seminar/stnless3.htm">Lesson 3:</a> Search Engines and Reference Collections: A Recommended List<p>
<li><a href="http://129.71.46.56/seminar/stnless4.htm">Lesson 4:</a> Search Strategies: Planning Your Search<p>
<li><a href="http://129.71.46.56/seminar/stnless5.htm">Lesson 5:</a> Evaluating and Citing Internet Resources
</ul>
<P>

<hr>
If you wish to test your newly-acquired skills, you may complete the
<a href="http://129.71.46.56/seminar/gradasgn.htm">graduation assignment</a>. <i>Try it out!</i><P>
<P>
Thanks for taking part, and if there's a question or a comment, please e-mail me or put it
on FSCNET-L.<P>
<P>
John J. Burke, MSLS
Librarian and Instructor
Ruth Ann Musick Library
Fairmont State College
jjb@fscvax.wvnet.edu
<a href="mailto:u536a@wvnvm.wvnet.edu">u536a@wvnvm.wvnet.edu</a>
<P>
Back to the <a href="http://129.71.46.56/two.html">Internet Resources</a> page.<p>
Last updated 11-19-96
<P>
</HTML>

Lesson 1

<HTML>
<body background="http://129.71.46.56/images/paper3.gif">
<center>
Searching the Net: Fall 1996<P><hr>
<P>
Lesson #1:
What Are You Looking For?<P>
" . . . seek and ye shall find . . . "
-- Matthew 7:7<P><p></center>

It's crucial to have your topic clearly in mind before you even begin searching the Net.
Through defining your topic and then refining it to make it more specific, you can find the
information you need. This lesson seeks to prove the point that while you may know what
you're looking for, you may not know how to express it in a manner to make your search
successful.<P>
Let's say I'm thinking of going on a trip to Barbados (yeah, right) and I would like to
check the Net for a little pre-trip planning information. In the Library, we suggest that
you start your search by writing out your information need as a sentence. For example, I
would write: "I need information about taking a trip to Barbados."<P>
Next, I would look at the sentence above and decide which of the words or phrases in it

were most important to my search. These search terms or keywords (the words and
phrases) are essential to the actual searching process, but they are also crucial to defining
and refining your topic. The keywords I see in my sentence are "Barbados" and "trip."
<P>
Now, I can go ahead and start using these terms in my search and see what happens.
Maybe I'll find a lot of sites on the Net, and maybe I won't. To better your chances of the
former, you should take some time now to refine your search. There are several ways to
do so.<P>
One thing to think about is whether or not your search is specific enough. If I had just
chosen "Barbados" as my lone keyword, for instance, I might find that I'll have to wade
through a lot of Net information before I locate information on trips. If you only find a
single keyword in your sentence, then think about these possible ways to make your
search more specific:<P>
<ul>
<li>a) Time: "Barbados" and "spring" or, historically, "Barbados" and "1700s"<P>
<li>b) Place: "Barbados" and "Bridgetown" (the capital)<P>
<li>c) Person or Group: "Barbados" and "tourists"<P>
<li>d) Event: "Barbados" and "discovery"<P>
<li>e) Aspect: "Barbados" and "exchange rate" or "Barbados" and "restaurants" <P>
</ul>
I already have used an aspect to refine my search ("Barbados" and "trip") so I'm ready to
move on. Another way to refine is to think of alternate terms or synonyms that you could
use in place of the keywords you've chosen. For instance, instead of "Barbados" I could
use "West Indies" or "Caribbean" as more general terms if I couldn't find enough
information on Barbados by itself. I could also use the word "trips" along with "trip"
since that word might appear in the plural. I could express the idea "trip" as "vacation" or
"travel." Eventually, I could look for more specific terms around the idea of a "trip," such
as "restaurants" or "hotels." If there were another name for the island of Barbados (a
synonym) I could use it as well.<P>
At the end of all this refining, you should have two things: the original sentence you
wrote down which explains what you need and a list of possible search terms. My
example would look like this:<P>

"I need information about taking a trip to Barbados."<P>
Search terms: Barbados, Caribbean, West Indies, trip, trips, vacation, travel, cruise,
cruises<P>

So now we're ready to go, but where to? Where do we begin searching? Better yet, can
we even expect to find the information I need on the Net? This final question will be
answered in our next lesson.<P>
I encourage you to try following the steps I've outlined above with your own information
need. If you start out with an example that's real to you, it will make the entire set of
lessons more useful. Or, you can just play along with my sample search and use these
lessons as reference points for future searching.<P>
Onward, ho!<P>
<p>
To <A HREF = "http://129.71.46.56/seminar/stnless2.htm">Lesson #2</A><P>
Back to the <A HREF = "http://129.71.46.56/seminar/stnintro.htm">Searching the Internet</A> page <P>
</HTML

Lesson 2

<HTML>
<body background="http://129.71.46.56/images/paper3.gif">

Searching the Net: Fall 1996<P><hr>
<P>
Lesson #2:
What Information Is Out There?
<P>
" . . . you shall seek all day ere you find them,
and, when you have them, < br>
they are not worth the search."
-- Shakespeare, The Merchant of Venice, 1596-1597
<P> <p>
Hopefully, the information you find on the Net won't take you all day to find and, most
importantly, will be worth the search. One way of ensuring these outcomes is to head to
the Net with a reasonable expectation that the information you need will actually be there.
Now, speaking as a librarian, let me tell you that useful information can exist in the
unlikeliest sources and the least expected places. I would never tell you to not look at the
Net, since it changes every day. However, there are some types of information that are

better bets than others.<P>
First, the good bets. The following is a list of kinds of
information that are well
represented online:<P>
<UL>
<LI>Answers to practical questions -- for example, a list of
frequently asked questions about <A HREF =
"http://tile.net:80/news/recs46.html">scuba diving.</A>
<LI>Product recommendations -- commonly appear in discussion
groups, such as rec.scuba, whose FAQ
appears at the link above.
<LI>E-mail addresses -- for example, see the list of
institutional phonebooks at <A HREF =
"gopher://gopher.nd.edu">Notre Dame University</A> (choose
"Non-Notre Dame Information Sources",
and then "Phone Books-Other Institutions."
<LI>U.S. government information -- an example would be the
Library of Congress' <A HREF =
"http://thomas.loc.gov">Thomas</A> Web site.
<LI>Company information -- for example, the <A HREF =
"http://www.toyota.com">Toyota </A> Web
page
<LI>Location-specific information -- for example, the Web page
for <A HREF =
"http://www.acadia.net/anp/"> Acadia National Park</A> in Maine
<LI>Specialized subject information -- such as <A HREF =
"http://www.lawguru.com:80/lawlinks.html">Lawguru.com</A> , a
legal information source collection.
<LI>Statistics -- the <A HREF =
"http://www.census.gov:80/main/www/srchtool.html">U.S. Bureau of
the Census</A> is a great example of a statistical source.
<LI>Electronic versions of print documents -- a collection of
these online books can be found at <A HREF
= "http://www.cs.cmu.edu/Web/books.html">Carnegie Mellon
University</A> .
<LI>Library holdings -- online library catalogs, such as the one
at the <A HREF =
"telnet://opac.lib.utk.edu">University of Tennessee</A> .
<LI>Information about the Net itself -- no shortage of this, such
as my own <A HREF =
"http://wvnvm.wvnet.edu/~u536a/lessons.html">Internet lessons</A>
.
<LI>"Ready-Reference" information -- a library science term for
brief, factual information, such as can be
found at the <A HREF = "http://k12.oit.umass.edu/rref.html">Ready
Reference Using the Internet</A>
site.
</UL>
<p>
Now, any list of what can be found on the Net begs the question
of what cannot be found.
Let me suggest to you that what the Net lacks more than anything
is an abundance of
easily available, substantial, and, last but not least, factual

information (regardless of
topic). Searching the Net is not the same as searching an
encyclopedia or searching a
periodical index. You never know what you will uncover on a
subject. This can be
exciting if you come across information that might not exist in a
magazine or journal or
encyclopedia article (or even a book!). It can also be
disheartening when you search and
search and find nothing useful.<P>
In order for the Net to be a "perfect" information source, it
needs to improve a lot. If this
improvement were to happen, I have no doubt that it would cost so
much that none of us
could afford a single search. For now, we should be happy that
we get what we get, but
remember that we get what we pay for sometimes (which is often
nothing).<P>
All this said, let me say a word about the two major formats of
information available on
the Net. First, we have "passive" sources, which are Web pages
or databases or online
collections of reference sources. These sources could be
compared to books or
periodicals in a library: they sit there, basically unchanging
or slowly changing, waiting for
us to search them. They make up the bulk of Net sources.<P>
"Active," on the other hand, is the name I give to sources that
are constantly in motion,
changing topic rapidly, never being quite the same at the end of
the day as they were at the
start. Electronic discussion groups, Usenet newsgroups, and chat
sessions are the best
examples of these sources. When the passive sources fail you,
you can turn to one of the
actives to ask a question that, hopefully, someone in the group
will answer for you.
Someone may at least suggest a passive source for you to look at.
My thought here is that
while we depend on passive sources on the Net (and in the real
world), the Net is designed
for person to person communication. You can try to run your
question past some living
information sources: the individuals who belong to the group.
<P>
Let's say you think the information you need could be out there.
Where can you look?
Rock on, good citizen, to Lesson #3.<P><p>
To <A HREF = "http://129.71.46.56/seminar/stnless3.htm">Lesson
#3</A> <P>
Back to the <A HREF =
"http://129.71.46.56/seminar/stnintro.htm">Searching the
Internet</A> page<P>
 <P>

```
</HTML>
```

Lesson 3

```
<HTML>
<body background="http://129.71.46.56/images/paper3.gif">
<center>
Searching the Net: Fall 1996<p><hr>
<p>
Lesson #3:<br>
Search Engines and Reference Collections:<br>
A Recommended List<p>

"Knowledge is of two kinds: we know a subject ourselves,<br>
 or we know where we can find information upon it."<br>
-- Samuel Johnson, Boswell's Life of Johnson, April 18,
1775<p><p>
</center>
So where can you search for your information? The problem is,
there are too many places to look. This lesson examines some Net
sources (active and passive) that I recommend using. They can be
organized into four categories. Below I have listed the address
and a link to each source along with an explanation of the
source's strengths and weaknesses.
<p>
<p>
Guides to Net Sources
<p>
Clearinghouse for Subject-Oriented Internet Resource Guides<br>
<A HREF =
"http://www.clearinghouse.net">http://www.clearinghouse.net</A>
<br>
This site is an ever-growing collection of guides written by Net
users and students at the University of Michigan's School of
Information Sciences. Each guide focuses on a certain topic, and
lists various sources that may be useful when searching for
information on the topic. Take a look at this site to see if
your topic is contained in a guide. You could also look to see
if one of the guides covers my travel to Barbados question. <p>

<p>
Search Engines<p>

There are a large number of sites which contain software which
enables them to search most or part of the Net. They are known
as "search engines." Their differences are indicated within the
descriptions which accompany them. Each one includes help
information and searching tips at their sites.<p>

Yahoo!<br>
<A HREF = "http://yahoo.com">http://yahoo.com</A><br>
Yahoo! includes over 370,000 sites and organizes them by subject.
You can simply choose the subject area that best fits your topic
```

and then work through it to get to the sites you need. You can
also use the search blank at the top of every Yahoo! page to
enter your topic, click on the word "Search," and then receive a
listing of sites in Yahoo! that fit your topic.<p>

WebCrawler
<A HREF = "http://webcrawler.com">http://webcrawler.com</A>
WebCrawler gives you a ranked listing of Web sites that match
your topic. It includes approximately 420,000 Web sites. You
can use the search blank on the main screen to search the full
grouping of sites or you can browse the GNN Select service, which
organizes reviews of individual sites by subject category.<p>

Open Text
<A HREF = "http://www.opentext.com">http://www.opentext.com</A>

Open Text works very similarly to WebCrawler, but it includes 5
million Web sites.<p>

Lycos
<A HREF = "http://www.lycos.com">http://www.lycos.com</A>
Lycos allows searching similar to that of WebCrawler or Open
Text, but it searches even more of the Web. Approximately 19
million Web sites and files are included in its database. It
also has a "Sites By Subject" option which is set up much like
Yahoo!<p>

InfoSeek
<A HREF =
"http://guide.infoseek.com">http://guide.infoseek.com</A>
InfoSeek works like the earlier engines and uses a search blank.
It includes about 1 million Web sites and, for something
completely different, messages from 10,000 Usenet newsgroups.
These groups include discussions on a wide variety of topics.
InfoSeek also lists sites from its most popular topics by
category. This is set up like Yahoo!, but is much more
limited.<p>

excite! NetSearch
<A HREF = "http://www.excite.com">http://www.excite.com</A>
excite! works on the InfoSeek model with 11.5 million Web sites
and 10,000 Usenet newsgroups.<p>

Alta Vista
<A HREF =
"http://altavista.digital.com"> http://altavista.digital.com</A>

Alta Vista is reputedly the most complete search engine on the
Net. It includes over 30 million Web sites and 13,000 Usenet
newsgroups. It has simple and advanced searching features, both
of which provide a search blank for you to enter your topic.<p>
Some useful tips for searching Alta Vista are the following: (1)
to be sure that each word you enter is included in the search,
precede that word with a + sign (i.e., +trips + barbados). (2) to

exclude any words from your search, precede those words with a -
sign (i.e., +trips +barbados -surfing). (3) to search for a
phrase, put quotes around it (i.e., "hang ten"). (4) to truncate
a word, which allows you to search for both a word and its
plural, put an * at the end of the word (i.e., trip* will find
"trip" or "trips"). Some of these features can be found on other
search engines in their help documentation.<p>

MetaCrawler
<A HREF = "http://metacrawler.cs.washington.edu:8080/">
http://metacrawler.cs.washington.edu:8080/ </A> < br>
If you haven't had enough of searching already, then MetaCrawler
is for you. It will do a combined search of eight other search
engines. Just enter your topic once and MetaCrawler will do the
work for you.<p>

Savvy Search
<A HREF =
"http://guaraldi.cs.colostate.edu:2000">http://guaraldi.cs.colost
ate.edu:2000</A>
If you really, really want to see nearly everything on the Web
under your topic, connect to Savvy Search. It searches
twenty-three search engines once you enter a topic. You may find
that you get too many results to handle if your topic is well
represented on the Net. If so, you should go back to the top of
the search engine list and try one of the less complete search
engines.<p>
Whew! That's a lot of choices in search engines! The next
lesson will try to help you narrow down your choices among them.
Let me just mention one site that has links to most of these
search engines and some other search devices. It may be of use
to you as a starting point for your searching.<p>

Browsing and Searching Internet Resources
<A HREF =
"http://www.ub2.lu.se/nav_menu.html">http://www.ub2.lu.se/nav_men
u.html</A> <p>
<p>

Ready-Reference Collections<p>

Internet Public Library Reference Collection
<A HREF =
"http://ipl.sils.umich.edu/ref/index.text.html"> http://ipl.sils.u
mich.edu/ref/index.text.html</A>
A collection of useful reference sources arranged by topic.
Everything from a dictionary of American Sign Language terms to a
directory of physicians organized by medical specialty can be
found here.<p>

Ready Reference Using the Internet
<A HREF =
"http://k12.oit.umass.edu/rref.html">http://k12.oit.umass.edu/rre

f.html</A>
This site has is a collection of sites which include brief bits
of factual information on a variety of topics. Select the
category that best fits your topic and see what the site can
offer. <p>
<p>

Directories of Active Sources<p>

Liszt Search
<A HREF =
"http://scwww.ucs.indiana.edu/mlarchive/"> http://scwww.ucs.indian
a.edu/mlarchive/</A>
A directory of electronic discussion groups (over 3000) which is
searchable by keyword or can be browsed alphabetically.<p>

Usenet Newsgroups atTile.net
<A HREF =
"http://www.tile.net/tile/news/index.html"> http://www.tile.net/ti
le/news/index.html</A>
A directory of Usenet Newsgroups which can be searched by
keyword. This is a helpful site for identifying newsgroups on a
topic, but you will need to check the availability of Usenet from
your individual account (Tile.net does not provide direct links
to the groups unless you already have a newsreader in your
account -- if these terms are unclear to you, see the lesson I
wrote on <A HREF =
"http://wvnvm.wvnet.edu/~u536a/lesson6.html">Usenet</A>). <p>
<p>

Searching Practice Time<p>

Now would probably be a good time for you to familiarize yourself
with a few of these sources by trying out a search or two.
Please use your own topic if you've defined one already,
otherwise you can use my "Barbados and trips" example. Get
together your list (or my list) of terms, and try out some
searches on the sources above. <p>

Let me suggest the following to you as you form your searches.
Many of the search engines and other sources above will allow for
Boolean searching by keyword. If you're not familiar with this
term, let me briefly define it as a method to link search terms
together for a more precise search. With the searches you will
be doing on the Net, you will want precision (since there are so
many documents and sites out there). My recommendation is that
you link your search terms together using a Boolean "and." All
this means is that if you're looking for information on
"Barbados" and information on "trips," you should enter your
search as: "Barbados and trips." Some of the search engines
will assume that you meant to put the word "and" in between your
terms even if you do not type it. Others will instead place the
Boolean "or" between your words, meaning that your search will
return documents or sites with either of the two or more words

you typed. To play it safe, go ahead and type the "and." If
you're interested in making your searches even more precise, look
at the help information available with the source to see what
options are available.
<p>
So try out a few searches to get the hang of it, and then get
ready to find the information you need. But where do you begin?
The next lesson suggests how to plan your search for maximum
efficiency and success.
<p>
<p>
To <A HREF = "http://129.71.46.56/seminar/stnless4.htm">Lesson
#4</A> <p>
Back to the <A HREF =
"http://129.71.46.56/seminar/stnintro.htm">Searching the
Internet</A> page

</HTML>

Lesson 4
_____

<HTML>
<body background="http://129.71.46.56/images/paper3.gif">

Searching the Net: Fall 1996<p>
<hr><p>
Lesson #4:
Search Strategies: Planning Your Search<p>

"Attempt the end, and never stand to doubt;
nothing's so hard but search will find it out."
-- Robert Herrick, "Seek and Find", Hesperides, 1648<p>

Your search will succeed once: a) your information need is
defined and refined, b) you know how to use the sources, and c)
you know what source to start with (and which ones to try next).
Having a plan before starting your search is essential, whether
you're finding information on the Net or in a library. Below I
discuss some issues to consider when planning your search and I
recommend some search strategies to use.<p>

As I said back in Lesson #1, you generally want to make your
search as specific (or, said another way, as precise) as
possible. That is, don't just look for information on
"Barbados," look for information on "Barbados and trip" (or "and
travel", etc.). There will, however, be times when this approach
simply does not work. The level of precision you have chosen for
the search may be too specific for the information that is
actually out there. For instance, let's say that I search for
"Barbados and restaurants" and find nothing. Maybe there are no
sites in the search engines or other sources that specify
"restaurants" as part of the information they include. I could

try returning to a less specific search ("Barbados and travel")
or even to a much more general search ("Barbados"). Of course,
your search's level of precision will affect how you proceed, and
this is discussed below. You need to be flexible in your
searching; always ready to try a new formation of search terms or
a new strategy.<p>

Now that we've talked a bit about how to express your search and
also how to come up with alternate terms to use, you should be
ready to handle the exciting world of searching for information.
The following lists are search strategies (ordered lists of
sources) that I have composed from the sources we discussed in
Lesson #3. Each strategy is written for a certain level of
precision that a search could have. While these strategies are
not perfect, they should get you started with your searching.
<p><p>

General Topic<p>
This strategy is for when an information need cannot be made more
specific or when a more specific search has failed. Examples of
this type of search would be searches such as:<p>
"I'd like to know what the Internet has in the field of
architecture."
"I need to find information about cancer." <p>
The strategy to follow is:
<ul>
<li><A HREF = "http://www.clearinghouse.net">The Clearinghouse
for
Subject-Oriented Internet Resource Guides</A>
<li><A HREF = "http://yahoo.com">Yahoo!</A>
<li>The GNN Select Service on <A HREF =
"http://webcrawler.com">WebCrawler</A>
<li>The "Sites by Subject" option on <A HREF =
"http://www.lycos.com">Lycos</A> </ul><p><p>

Specific Topic<p>
This strategy will be used when you have a more specific search
in mind. Examples would be:<p>
"I would like information on taking a trip to Barbados."
"I need to know something about the construction of bridges."<p>
I suggest that you move from sources that are a little more
manageable in size to ones that are larger until you have
exhausted the Web search engines. The strategy to follow
is:
<ul>
<li><A HREF = "http://yahoo.com">Yahoo!</A>
<li><A HREF = "http://webcrawler.com">WebCrawler</A>
<li><A HREF = "http://www.opentext.com">Open Text</A> or <A HREF
= "http://guide.infoseek.com">InfoSeek</A> or <A HREF =
"http://www.excite.com">excite!</A>
<li><A HREF = "http://www.lycos.com">Lycos</A> or <A HREF =
"http://altavista.digital.com">Alta Vista</A> (Web search and
Usenet search)
<li><A HREF = "http://guaraldi.cs.colostate.edu:2000">Savvy
Search</A> or <A HREF =
"http://metacrawler.cs.washington.edu:8080/">MetaCrawler</A>

<li><A HREF =
"http://ipl.sils.umich.edu/ref/index.text.html">Internet Public
Library Reference Collection</A> or <A HREF =
"http://k12.oit.umass.edu/rref.html">Ready Reference Using the
Internet</A> </ul><p><p>

Specific Question<p>
This strategy fits two general situations: a) where you need a
fact of some sort, and b) where you need to find a specific
product or organization or individual. Examples would be:<p>
"I need to know the population of Shanghai."
"I need to know something about Hewlett Packard Laserjet
printers."<p>
For the first question, I recommend trying ready-reference
collections (as listed above) and then trying search engines. As
a last resort, you could put your question to a discussion group
or newsgroup.
For questions like the latter, I would suggest using active
sources over passive ones if the question involves a practical
question (whether to buy an HP Laserjet). Otherwise, I would use
Alta Vista or Yahoo! to locate the organization or individual.
The strategy would be:
<ul>
<li><A HREF = "http://scwww.ucs.indiana.edu/mlarchive/">Liszt
Search</A> or <A HREF =
"http://www.tile.net/tile/news/index.html">Usenet Newsgroups at
Tile.net</A> (to find an appropriate discussion group or
newsgroup)
<li><a href="http://altavista.digital.com">Alta Vista</a>
(Usenet and Web)
<li><a href="http://yahoo.com">Yahoo!</a></ul><p><p>

Now you should have some idea of how to start looking for the
information you need. Give it a try with your search terms or
with my example. See what you think of the strategies and feel
free to make suggestions to improve them. You can be assured
that you will find information now. How can you decide if it's
worthy of use? What do you do to refer to an information source
in a publication of your own? Read on.<p><p>
 To <A HREF = "http://129.71.46.56/seminar/stnless5.htm">Lesson
#5<p>
</A>
Back to the <A HREF =
"http://129.71.46.56/seminar/stnintro.htm">Searching the
Internet</A> page
</HTML>

Lesson 5

<HTML>
<body background="http://129.71.46.56/images/paper3.gif">
<center>
Searching the Net: Fall 1996<p>
<hr><p>

Lesson #5:
Evaluating and Citing Internet Resources<p>

"The search is over . . . "
-- Survivor, 1985<p></center>

This lesson is designed to help you with two practical needs.
First, you will want to examine the information you've found on
the Net and decide if it is credible or useful for your needs.
Second, if you decide to use a source you find on the Net in a
paper or other work that you create, you will need to know how to
give credit to the source's creator. I hope that this will get
you thinking about the quality of information on the Net and will
remind you of your responsibility to give credit where credit is
due.<p>
<p>
Evaluating Net Information<p>

The information that ends up on the Net runs the gamut from
authoritative facts to "one person's opinion" to unadulterated
propaganda or misinformation. Because the Net is an ever-growing,
more or less egalitarian communications medium, anyone out there
is free to put up any information they wish. While as a whole
this is a good idea (a networked community can share a lot of
useful information), we need to be cautious about the information
we find. When you find a site on the Net which has interesting
or useful information on it, you can run down this checklist of
questions to help you evaluate the site.<p>
<ul>
<li>
Who put this information here? Does the site represent the
findings of a scholarly research team or the musings of your
average Joe? Basically, how authoritative can we expect the
source to be based on the credentials of its creator(s)? A site
listing hotel and motel rates put together by the National
Tourism Council of Barbados can usually be trusted more than John
Q. Public's "My Trip to Barbados." <p>
<li>Where did the creator(s) get the information? A published
source or sources? No cited sources? Whether it's a new cure
for cancer or a list of concert dates, you want to have some
confidence that its accurate.<p>
<li>Is the information biased in any way? Can you detect a
particular slant that the site is pushing? While this factor
does not always invalidate the information found at the site, it
should cause you to find other objective sources to verify the
information.<p>
<li>Is the information current enough for your need? Is there a
date of creation given on the site's pages? You'd hate to be
representing the population of Panama as a certain number (taken
from a 1980 census) when the most current number (a 1994 census)
was much higher. <p>
<li>Will the site be there next time I log in? This is hard to
judge, but if you are going to cite the information from a site,
you hope that it will be around for others to see. If a site

appears to be updated often or is represented by an organization of some sort, chances are it will be around for a while. Sadly, many brilliant sites by college students disappear when the semester ends or graduation day comes.<p>
<li>How does the information presented compare with other sources (either on the Net or at the Library)? If something strikes you as fishy, you may want to give the Library a call or drop by and let us help you confirm it using other sources. Some information, however, exists only on the Net and cannot be easily verified elsewhere.<p>
</ul>
These questions will get you started in evaluating Net sites. For a sense of what some non- (or perhaps in-) credible sites look like, try the following one on <A HREF = "http://147.129.1.10/library/lib2/AIDSFACTS.html">AIDS Facts</A> . The link at the bottom of that document takes you to a page with more details on the evaluation of Net information.<p>
<p>
Citing the Sites<p>

The issue of representing these Net sites in the confines of a research paper or other publication is a confusing one. While many new editions of style manuals include suggested citation formats for online information sources, they often leave out the type of site you need to site (i.e., the newest edition (10th) of the MLA Handbook for Writers of Research Papers covers electronic mail messages very well, but leaves out World Wide Web sites). Folks on the Net have come up with solutions to this problem, suggesting methods of citation that are derived from the various manuals. <p>

One site that I like for MLA or other usage is this one put together by <A HREF = "http://www.nueva.pvt.k12.ca.us/~debbie/library/research/research.html">Debbie Abilock</A> . She has set up a page with examples of MLA style citations for various types of Net sites. She also has a set of forms which let you enter the pertinent information about a site and then create a citation for you. Try it out!<p>

For those of you who prefer APA style, Xia Li and Nancy Crane have a set of templates and sample citations on their page at the <A HREF = "http://www.uvm.edu/%7Exli/reference/apa.html">University of Vermont</A> . They have also written a book entitled The Official Internet World Guide to Electronic Styles: A Handbook to Citing Electronic Information. Meckler, 1996. An earlier version of this work is located at the Ruth Ann Musick Library Reference Desk.<p>

The basic idea of citing sources is to give added credibility to your own work and to lead your readers on to other useful sources. You should feel confident in including Internet sites in your work, so long as you evaluate them first and then cite them correctly.<p>

<p>
Conclusion<p>

These five lessons have provided you with a foothold to begin searching the Internet more effectively. There are countless other guides and resources that may be of help to you in your searching, and please feel free to ask me for other suggestions. You may of course, wish to try searching for them yourself using the sites and strategies suggested above. <p>

I must thank the Ruth Ann Musick Library for the opportunity to bring these lessons to you. They were inspired by the work of myself and my colleagues in the Library as we attempted to help people find much needed information on the Net. I also wish to cite two sources that I drew upon for these lessons:<p>

Grassian, Esther. (1996, May 9). Thinking Critically About World Wide Web Resources [Online]. Available: http://www.ucla.edu:80/bruinonline/trainers/critical.html [1996, May 9].<p>

Staines, Gail. (1996, June 3). Summary: Evaluation of 'Net Sources Workshop. Internet/BITNET Network Trainers [Online]. Available E-mail: nettrain@ubvm.cc.buffalo.edu [1996, June 3].<p>

If you are interested in testing your skills in searching, then go on to the <A HREF = "http://129.71.46.56/seminar/gradasgn.html">graduation assignment</A>.<p>
Back to the <A HREF = "http://129.71.46.56/seminar/stnintro.htm">Searching the Internet</A> page.
</html>

Notes:

WWW Basics; An Introductory Workshop

BRUCE HARLEY
Associate Librarian, Government Publications & Maps Division
SAN DIEGO STATE UNIVERSITY

CIRCUMSTANCES FOR THE INSTRUCTION SESSION:

In the Fall of 1993, there was no campus-wide instruction in the use of the Internet at San Diego State University (SDSU). Given the publicity the Internet was already receiving and its implications for Library services, I was asked by the Library's Information & Collection Services Director to develop a program of Internet instruction for the SDSU community. Serving in my capacity as Coordinator of Library Electronic Information Services, I formed a working group of "volunteer" librarians to develop this program. In the Spring and Fall of 1994, several librarians participated in a program of workshops which consisted of modules on telnet (featuring OPACS, gopher, WAIS and the WWW via Lynx), electronic mail and File Transfer Protocol. Instruction was done in library classrooms, each of which was equipped with a networked instructor's workstation and projection system.

In 1995, we made the WWW the focus of the instructional workshops, made Netscape our WWW browser of choice and also made copies of handouts for these workshops available on the Library's new webserver. In the Fall of 1996, the Library's new electronic classrooms equipped with instructor AND attendees' workstations as well as improved projection systems were used for the WWW workshops for the first time. Response to the workshops has been positive since their inception. Demand for the workshops is still high although attendance has declined. The Library is no longer unique in offering Internet/WWW instruction and many faculty, staff and students we have taught have no doubt taught other campus community members on their own.

See the section on CIRCUMSTANCES FOR THE INSTRUCTION SECTION in the chapter entitled "AN ADVANCED WORLD WIDE WEB (WWW) WORKSHOP: Searching the Internet" for more on the development of San Diego State University Library's Internet instructional program.

OBJECTIVES OF THE INSTRUCTION:

There are several teaching/learning objectives for the introductory WWW workshop. Upon completion of one of these workshops, attendees should be familiar with:

- different approaches to **Learning About the WWW**, including instruction offered at SDSU and resources available online;
- the relationship between **The WWW and the Internet**;

- **WWW Characteristics**, especially:
    - a. **standards—HTTP, HTML & URLs**,
    - b. **Internet functions,**
    - c. **hypermedia display formats, and**
    - d. **networked information search tools**.
- **WWW Access**, especially:
    - a. **WWW Browser (Netscape) features,**
    - b. **Levels of WWW Access at SDSU, and**
    - c. **SDSU Computer Accounts**.
- questions to be asked when **Evaluating WWW Sources of Information**;
- the issue of **WWW Documents & Copyright**; and
- where to get help **Citing WWW Documents**.

COMPONENTS OF THE LIBRARY INSTRUCTION:

A focus of the introductory WWW workshop is to demonstrate how the WWW can be self-teaching. This is done in part by having the two handouts listed below accessible via the WWW by all attendees at these workshops:

- "THE WORLD WIDE WEB (WWW)"
    http://libweb.sdsu.edu/gov/wwwdos.html and
- "SEARCH THE WORLD WIDE WEB (WWW)"
    http://libweb.sdsu.edu/gov/search.html

Attendees follow librarians' opening lectures by referring to the printed copies of the handouts and also get hands-on experience as part of structured WWW presentations. Text-only versions of both handouts are included in this chapter.

PART I INTRODUCTION (Lecture; 15 minutes)

During the first 15 minutes, the librarian:
1. introduces her/himself as a librarian and informs attendees where in the Library they can access the WWW;
2. draws attendees' attention to the type of hardware and software they will be using and encourages those familiar with Windows or Macintosh to help their less experienced "networked neighbors;"
3. informs attendees that they will be asked to complete an evaluation form at the completion of the workshop;
4. assures attendees that there will be time for questions and answers at the end of the workshop but that it is also OK to ask questions before then; and
5. provides an overview of the contents of the handouts, especially the sections on:
    a. different approaches to LEARNING ABOUT THE WWW, including instruction offered at SDSU and resources available online;
    b. the relationship between

c. WWW Access;
    1. WWW Browsers, including Netscape;
    2. Levels of WWW Access at SDSU; and
    3. SDSU Computer Accounts.

PART II WWW BASICS (Lecture/Hands-On Activity; 65 minutes)

During the next 65 minutes, the librarian lectures briefly on WWW basics while giving attendees ample opportunities for hands-on activities. Attendees are first asked to run Netscape on their workstations. The "home page" designated for these workstations is the Library's welcome page @ http://libweb.sdsu.edu/. Once the connection has been made, they are directed to the online copy of "THE WORLD WIDE WEB (WWW)" @ http://libweb.sdsu.edu/gov/wwwdos.html.

The outline presented below can be followed in order to give workshop attendees a guided tour of selected Netscape features and, at the same time, introduce them to **WWW CHARACTERISTICS** associated with the selected features, especially:

    1. standards - HTTP, HTML & URLs;
    2. Internet functions;
    3. hypermedia display formats; and
    4. networked information search tools.

Lecture Outline for: WWW Basics; An Introductory Workshop

I.   **Netscape menus and toolbar** [Attendees should be viewing the first screen of "THE WORLD WIDE WEB (WWW)" @ http://libweb.sdsu.edu/gov/wwwdos.html (see text in handout included in this chapter)]
    A. Options menu
        1. Preferences
            a. General (including Home Page Location), Apps & Helpers
            b. Mail and News
        2. Show Toolbar, Location and Directory Buttons
        3. Auto Load Images (see II.C., hypermedia display formats, below)
    B. Directory menu
    C. Help menu
    D. Toolbar icons

II.   **WWW Characteristics**
    A. HTTP & HTML
       [Attendees should navigate to WWW CHARACTERISTICS #1 in "THE WORLD WIDE WEB (WWW)"]
        1. View menu
            a. Reload
            b. Source

2. File menu
    a. Mail Document
    b. Save As (see Open File) [vs. Save Image as...pop-up menu item—
      Librarian demonstrates right mouse click over Library logo "You'll Find It Under the Dome"]
    c. Print Preview and Print

B. URLs & Internet functions
    [Attendees should navigate to WWW CHARACTERISTICS #'s 1 & 2
    in "THE WORLD WIDE WEB (WWW)"]
    1. File menu
      a. Open Location
        [Attendees should open each of the following locations (or some other representative
locations)   in succession]
        1. gopher, e.g., gopher://marvel.loc.gov/
        2 (anonymous) FTP, e.g., ftp://rohan.sdsu.edu/
        3. telnet, e.g., telnet://library.sdsu.edu
        4. HTTP, e.g., http://libweb.sdsu.edu/gov/wwwdos.html
    2.Go menu
      a. Home (see I.A.1.a., above)
      b. Stop Loading
      c. history list (see Window/History, below)
    3. Window menu
      a. History (see Go/history list, above)
    4. File menu
      a. New Browser
    5. Bookmarks menu
      [Attendees should create one or more bookmarks, including one for "THE WORLD WIDE
      WEB (WWW)" to which they should return]
      a. Add Bookmark
      b. Go to Bookmarks
        1. File sub-menu
          a. Open
          b. Import
          c. Save-As
          d. What's New
        2. Item sub-menu
          a. Properties
C. Hypermedia display formats
    [The librarian demonstrates the following types of files .
    Attendees should navigate to WWW CHARACTERISTICS #3 in
    "THE WORLD WIDE WEB (WWW)"]
    1. Still Image (e.g., gif, jpeg); and
    2. Video/Audio (e.g., shockwave, quicktime [vr], vrml, java, realaudio).

D. Networked information search tools

[Attendees should navigate to

WWW CHARACTERISTICS in "THE WORLD WIDE WEB (WWW)"]

1. Edit menu

    a. Find

2. Search the World Wide Web

[Attendees should be reviewing the first screen of "SEARCH THE WORLD WIDE WEB"

@ http://libeb.sdsu.edu/gov/search.html (text of handout included in this

chapter)]

    a. Search **this** WWW Server

[Attendees should follow this link and perform a search of all WWW documents on

Libweb, then return to "SEARCH THE WORLD WIDE WEB"]

    b. Search **all SDSU** WWW Servers

[Attendees should follow this link and perform a search of all WWW documents on

WWW servers at SDSU, then return to "SEARCH THE WORLD WIDE WEB

(WWW)"]

    c. Search WWW servers **around the world**

[Attendees should navigate to each of the following sections of "SEARCH THE WORLD

WIDE WEB (WWW)" in succession. They will be asked to perform a search using

a site listed under HTTP Catalog, HTTP Catalogs/Indexes, HTTP Indexes and HTTP Indexes:

Simultaneous, Integrated Searching. The librarian may demonstrate additional sites]

        1. HTTP Search Sites

            a. HTTP Catalog

            b. HTTP Catalogs/Indexes

            c. HTTP Catalogs/Indexes and Reviews

            d. HTTP Indexes

            e. HTTP Catalogs/Indexes: Multiple Links

            f. HTTP Indexes: Simultaneous, Integrated Searching

        2. GOPHER Search Sites

        3. FTP Search Sites

        4. TELNET Search Site

        5. News Search Sites

        6. Mailing List Search Sites

        7. White Pages Search Site

3. Directory menu

    a. Internet Search

    b. People

4. WWW Cataloging and Search Agents [The librarian briefly describes:

    a. the META tag; WWW site promotion

    b. projects to catalog WWW resources (e.g., OCLC's InterCat and

       NetFirst); and

    c. personalized WWW search services—search agents or webcasters (e.g.,

       My Yahoo, PointCast)

III. **Evaluating WWW Sources of Information**

The librarian reviews the types of questions to be asked when interpreting search results or evaluating WWW information sources [Attendees should navigate to Evaluating WWW Sources of Information in "The World Wide Web (WWW)"]

IV.**WWW Documents & Copyright**

The librarian briefly reviews the issue of WWW documents and copyright [Attendees should navigate to WWW Documents & Copyright in "The World Wide Web (WWW)"]

V. **Citing WWW Documents**

The librarian briefly indicates where attendees can get online help citing WWW documents [Attendees should navigate to Citing WWW Documents in "The World Wide Web (WWW)"]

Part III Questions & Answers/Evaluation (10 minutes)

The librarian asks for questions and requests that attendees take a few minutes to fill out the "WWW Instruction Evaluation" form (included in this chapter and may be reproduced). The librarian also lets attendees know that she or he is available to meet with them individually.

Variations:

Librarians from other institutions can substitute appropriate alternatives for SDSU-specific content with regard to the Objectives of the Instruction and parts of the Components of the Library Instruction..

[Malcolm A. Love Library]   **THE WORLD WIDE WEB (WWW)**

Contents

    * LEARNING ABOUT THE WWW
    * THE WWW AND THE INTERNET
    * WWW CHARACTERISTICS
        o STANDARDS
            + HYPERTEXT TRANSFER PROTOCOL (HTTP)
            + HYPTERTEXT MARKUP LANGUAGE (HTML)
            + UNIFORM RESOURCE LOCATOR (URL)
        o INTERNET FUNCTIONS
        o HYPERMEDIA DISPLAY FORMATS
        o NETWORKED INFORMATION SEARCH TOOLS
    * WWW ACCESS
    * EVALUATING WWW SOURCES OF INFORMATION
    * WWW DOCUMENTS & COPYRIGHT
    * CITING WWW DOCUMENTS

LEARNING ABOUT THE WWW

The Library offers WWW instruction. Schedules are posted in the Library
lobby, in the Weekly and @ http://libweb.sdsu.edu/gov/addos.html.
Information on additional computing-related workshops, seminars, classes
and instructional materials is available @
http://rohan.sdsu.edu/workshop.html. Net-Happenings and The Scout-Report @
http://wwwscout.cs.wisc.edu/scout/index.html provide information on WWW
developments, as does InterNIC News @
http://rs.internic.net/nic-support/nicnews/.

THE WWW AND THE INTERNET

The WWW and the Internet are not synonymous. The Internet is the network of
computer networks, based on telecommunications protocols (or rules) which
enable different types of computers to exchange information. The WWW, based
on one of these protocols, is a system for structuring and finding Internet
resources.

WWW CHARACTERISTICS

    1. The WWW is based on the following standards:
        o HyperText Transfer Protocol (HTTP) makes possible the exchange of
          hypertext-based information. Hypertext-based information is
          presented in documents like this one which contain links to
          networked information resources. Hypertext documents are WWW
          documents.

o HyperText Markup Language (HTML) is used to create WWW documents. Hypertext provides authors of WWW documents with a non-linear presentation style. For information on HTML and creating WWW documents, see: http://www.sdsu.edu/developers/ and http://rohan.sdsu.edu/. See also the generally applicable sections in LIBWEB DOCUMENT GUIDELINES @ http://libweb.sdsu.edu/gov/guide.html.

o Uniform Resource Locators (URLs) are an addressing scheme for sources of networked information. The URL format is: <protocol>://<domain name>:<port>/<document path>/<file name>

+ Protocol:
A protocol is a computer language with a unique set of rules or grammar. Each protocol represents an Internet function, including: ftp (File Transfer Protocol), gopher, http (HyperText Transfer Protocol, for WWW documents), mailto (URL format = mailto:<address>), news (URL format = news:<newsgroup name>) and telnet.

+ Domain Name and Port:
A domain name, such as libweb.sdsu.edu, consists of a computer host or server name (e.g., libweb), an institutional identifier (e.g., sdsu) and an institutional type identifier (e.g., edu). You would use this domain name to connect to the computer named "libweb" at San Diego State University, an educational institution. To connect to "libweb" via the WWW you would use the following URL: http://libweb.sdsu.edu/
Sometimes you must specify a port number after a domain name to connect to a particular computer (e.g., gopher://honor.uc.wlu.edu:1020/).

+ Document Path and File Name:
The document path indicates the directory and subdirectory, if any, in which a file is stored. In the URL http://libweb.sdsu.edu/gov/wwwdos.html the file named "wwwdos.html" is stored in the "gov" directory on "libweb."

2. The WWW supports a variety of Internet functions, including anonymous File Transfer Protocol (FTP), gopher, HyperText Transfer Protocol (HTTP), mailto, news and telnet. You can use the WWW to transfer files, access a gopher site, access a WWW site, send a WWW document via e-mail, read Usenet newsgroups on a local news server and telnet to a remote computer.

3. The WWW supports a variety of hypermedia display formats of networked information, including still image file, video file, and audio file formats. You need a graphic-based WWW browser (see WWW ACCESS, below) to display these networked information formats. Graphic-based WWW browsers require at least Windows 3.1 for IBM-compatibles or Macintosh system 7.0. Networked information display formats require still image, video and audio applications or "viewers." A "viewer" may be a browser, a browser plug-in or a separate application that works with a browser.

4. The WWW supports a variety of networked information search tools, including WWW tools (manual- or list-based browsable catalogs - e.g., Yahoo; automated-or robot-based searchable indexes - e.g., InfoSeek and AltaVista), gopher indexes (Veronica and Jughead), HyTelnet (a guide to telnet resources) and Archie, an index of names of files available via anonymous FTP. No networked information search tool is comprehensive. Searching two or more of these tools may yield some duplication of results. Browsing WWW catalogs is recommended for general topics (e.g., anthropology, Peruvian archaeology). Searching WWW indexes is recommended for specific topics (e.g., San Diego Zoo). Networked information search tools can be evaluated on the basis of their:

> o scope of coverage (e.g., WWW files only vs. WWW and other files)
> o update frequency
> o search engine: breadth-first (e.g., top-level WWW documents) vs. depth-first (all WWW documents)
> o search content: titles/headings, brief descriptions, full text, URL's
> o search capabilities: approximate match, (explicit vs. implicit) logical/Boolean operators, proximity operators, truncation, phrase searching, searchable fields (e.g., title), searchable source features (e.g., location, media type)
> o search speed
> o search results display: excerpt/keyword-in-context or summary, scoring or ranking (i.e., relevance feedback), URLs, hot links
> o help: Frequently Asked Questions (FAQ), search samples, etc.

Additional information about searching and networked information search tools is provided by The Spider's Apprentice: How to Use Web Search Engines @ http://www.monash.com/spidap.html, The Matrix of Internet Catalogs and Search Engines @ http://www.ambrosiasw.com/~fprefect/matrix/, Scout Toolkit: Searching the Internet @ http://wwwscout.cs.wisc.edu/scout/toolkit/search/index.html and Search Helper: Windweaver's Easy Search @ http://www.windweaver.com/searchhelper.htm.

Selected local and remote WWW sites with networked information search tools are accessible @ http://libweb.sdsu.edu/gov/search.html.

BEGINNING OF DOCUMENT

WWW ACCESS

WWW Browsers

You access the WWW with either a text-based browser or graphic-based browser. A WWW browser is a software client application which enables you to access or browse the networked information comprising the WWW. This information is stored and managed by software server applications. Public domain freeware and shareware WWW browsers for IBM-compatibles and Macintoshes are available via anonymous FTP. For example, versions of

Netscape Navigator are available from http://home.netscape.com/ and http://rohan.sdsu.edu/Netscape.html for free to educational and nonprofit users and for unlimited evaluation use by others. Netscape is also available via SDSU AzNET Accounts. See http://www.znet.com/sdsu/ for more information (see Levels of WWW Access at SDSU, #3, and SDSU/ AzNET Computer Accounts, below).

Levels of WWW Access at SDSU

You may browse the WWW in a variety of ways, including the following which represent levels of access to the WWW:

1. via a graphic-based WWW browser on an IBM-compatible with Windows OR a Macintosh with a direct connection to the Internet from the Library, a computer lab or an office on campus.

2. via a graphic-based browser on an IBM-compatible with Windows OR a Macintosh connected to the Internet from off campus by an SDSU multi-user host computer accessible by telephone with a modem and communications software and on which you have an account. Free full WWW access applies to faculty and staff only; free student access is restricted to SDSU WWW sites. See SDSU/ AzNETComputer Accounts, below, and contact Telecommunications and Network Services (TNS) for additional information (Business Administration Building 116, 594-5261, http://tns.sdsu.edu/).

3. via zNET, a commercial Internet provider accessible by telephone. See http://www.znet.com/sdsu/ for more information. This applies especially to students, but faculty and staff can also purchase accounts. See SDSU/ AzNETComputer Accounts, below. If you are interested in commercial access to the Internet via a different provider, search Mecklermedia's The List @ http://thelist.iworld.com/, OR point your WWW browser @ http://www.crl.com/~wkronert/isp/service.html OR send the following message: send /faq/internic-provider-list to: mailserv@is.internic.net InterNIC may also be contacted at: 619-455-4600 (voice), 619-455-4640 (FAX), info@internic.net (email), http://rs.internic.net/ (WWW), gopher.internic.net (gopher), is.internic.net (telnet; login as "gopher") and is.internic.net (anonymous FTP).

4. via a text-based browser on an SDSU multi-user host computer attached to the Internet and on which you have an account. This level of WWW access can be attained by telephone, modem and communications software from off campus OR by direct Internet connection on campus. This applies to faculty and staff only.

The first, second and third levels of access provide alternative means of access to WWW functions resident on your own computer. The second and third levels of access approximate the first level of access. The fourth level of access provides a means of access to WWW functions resident on a computer you connect to remotely.

SDSU/AzNET Computer Accounts

To access the WWW remotely (i.e. off campus) via the second or fourth level, you will need an SDSU or AzNET computer account. First, if you are faculty or academic staff, you will need an account on rohan.sdsu.edu. This account will provide you with the fourth level of WWW access via Lynx. In addition, you will also need a Kerberos account. These accounts, used in conjunction with the appropriate communications software will provide you with the second level of WWW access. For more information on rohan accounts, see http://rohan.sdsu.edu/0500stud.html. For more information on kerberos accounts, contact Telecommunications and Network Services (TNS) (Business Administration Building 116, 594-5261, http://tns.sdsu.edu/). Second, if you are a student, you will need an AzNET account. This account will provide you with the third level of WWW access. For more information on AzNET accounts, see http://www.znet.com/sdsu/.

For the latest information on changes to remote WWW access by SDSU faculty, staff and students, see "SDSU Remote Access" @ http://tns.sdsu.edu/remote/aia.html.

BEGINNING OF DOCUMENT

EVALUATING WWW SOURCES OF INFORMATION

Esther Grassian, UCLA College Library, lists many points to consider when Thinking Critically about World Wide Web Resources @ http://www.library.ucla.edu/libraries/college/instruct/critical.htm. Jan Alexander and Marsha Tate provide "Web Evaluation Checklists" for advocacy, business/marketing, informational, news and personal home pages @ http://www.science.widener.edu/~withers/webeval.htm. Joan Ormondroyd, Michael Engle and Tony Cosgrave offer general suggestions on appraising and analyzing information sources @ http://www.library.cornell.edu/okuref/research/skill26.htm. For WWW source design considerations, see "Before you begin working on a document" in LIBWEB DOCUMENT GUIDELINES @ http://libweb.sdsu.edu/gov/guide.html. For a webliography of additional sites focused on evaluating WWW sources, see Information Quality WWW Virtual Library @ http://coombs.anu.edu.au/WWWVL-InfoQuality.html. For WWW sites that provide evaluations of WWW sources, see "HTTP Catalogs/Indexes and Reviews" under "HTTP SEARCH SITES" in Search the World Wide Web (WWW) @ http://libweb.sdsu.edu/gov/search.html.

Summarizing some of the sites listed above, the following questions should be asked when evaluating a WWW source:

  * Who is responsible for publishing the information provided by the
    source? What are the credentials and affiliation or sponsorship of any
    named individuals or organizations? How authoritative are they?
  * What can be said about the content, context, style, structure,
    completeness and accuracy of the information provided by the source?
    Are any conclusions offered? If so, based on what criteria and

supported by what secondary and primary documentation?
* When was the information provided by the source published? Is the
information provided by the source in its original form or has it been
revised? Is this information updated regularly?
* Where else can the information provided by the source be found on the
WWW? Is this information authentic? Is this information unique or has
it been copied?
* Why was the information provided by the source published? What are the
perspectives, opinions, assumptions and biases of whomever is
responsible for this information? Who is the intended audience?

WWW DOCUMENTS & COPYRIGHT

It has been suggested that you "[download] or print all documents you
intend to cite" and cite a printed version, whenever available, especially
if it is a primary or original source and contains "more information than
an abridged electronic version." (Arnzen, Michael. "Cyber Citations,"
Internet World. Vol. 7, No. 9., September, 1996, p. 72-74.) As for
downloading or printing WWW documents, assume that they are protected by
copyright unless they are declared to be in the public domain or a
copyright date has expired. "Single copies of short items for a person's
own study may fall within fair use." (CSU-SUNY-CUNY Joint Committee. Fair
Use of Copyrighted Works: A Crucial Element in Educating America, 1995, p.
24-25.)

CITING WWW DOCUMENTS

A variety of Citing Electronic Information style guides made be found @
http://libweb.sdsu.edu/cite.html.

BEGINNING OF DOCUMENT

The author of this document (URL = http://libweb.sdsu.edu/gov/wwwdos.html)
is Bruce Harley.
E-mail: harley@mail.sdsu.edu

Original HTML Markup by Jerry Palsson.

Previous page (Information by Subject), OR
Previous page (LIBWEB DOCUMENT GUIDELINES) OR
Previous page (Bruce Harley's home page)

Return to Library Home Page

Last change March 10, 1997.
webmaster@libweb.sdsu.edu

[Malcolm A. Love Library]   **SEARCH THE WORLD WIDE WEB (WWW)**

Search this WWW server @ http://libweb.sdsu.edu/Search.html

Search all SDSU WWW servers @ http://www.sdsu.edu/search/index.html

Search WWW servers around the world @...

Selected WWW Search Sites

HTTP | GOPHER | FTP | TELNET | NEWS | MAILING LISTS | WHITE PAGES

These WWW sites with search tools are arranged according to the primary
type of Internet function or protocol they support or provide information
on. Several of the search sites listed under HTTP (HyperText Transfer
Protocol) SEARCH SITES support or provide information on multiple Internet
functions. The HTTP SEARCH SITES are subdivided by sites that offer
browsable catalogs, sites that offer browsable catalogs and searchable
indexes, sites that also offer reviews, sites that offer searchable indexes
only, sites that provide links to multiple catalogs and indexes, sites that
provide simultaneous, integrated searching of multiple indexes, and other
WWW search sites. The URL's for all of these sites are subject to change.
Recommendations of HTTP search sites have been made by the author of this
document and are his alone. Examples of the search capabilities of these
sites are available @ http://libweb.sdsu.edu/gov/recommend.html.

Introductory information on networked information search tools is available
@ http://libweb.sdsu.edu/gov/wwwdos.html#search.

HTTP SEARCH SITES

HTTP Catalog

This site offers a browsable catalog that organizes WWW resources in broad
subject categories (good for locating general information).

  1. The WWW Virtual Library
     DESCRIPTION: "a distributed subject catalogue "
     URL: http://www.w3.org/pub/DataSources/bySubject/Overview.html

HTTP Catalogs/Indexes

These sites offer both browsable catalogs that organize WWW resources in
broad subject categories (good for locating general information) AND
searchable indexes or search "engines" (good for locating specific
information).

  1. Galaxy
     DESCRIPTION: browse the "Galaxy Directory" or search the Web, Galaxy
     Pages, Gopher Titles and Telnet Resources (see HyTelnet under TELNET
     SEARCH SITES, below)
     URL: http://galaxy.einet.net/

2. Infoseek [*recommended*] for the precise results retrieved by its
   index (see Alta Vista under HTTP Indexes, below)
   DESCRIPTION: browse topics or search the Web, Usenet Newsgroups, Web
   FAQ's and more via "Ultrasmart" or "Ultraseek"; see examples of search
   capabilities
   URL: http://guide.infoseek.com/

3. Yahoo [*recommended*] for its catalog DESCRIPTION: browse or search
   catalog topics; links to Alta Vista (see below) when searches retrieve
   zero results; see examples of search capabilities
   URL: http://www.yahoo.com/

HTTP Catalogs/Indexes and Reviews

In addition to catalogs and indexes, these sites also offer reviews of
selected WWW resources.

1. Excite
   DESCRIPTION: browse "Excite Web Reviews" or "Search the entire Web"
   URL: http://www.excite.com

2. Lycos
   DESCRIPTION: browse the "a2z Sites by Subject" or search "The Web";
   provides POINT reviews
   URL: http://lycos.cs.cmu.edu/

3. Magellan
   DESCRIPTION: "BROWSE TOPICS" or search either the "entire database" or
   just sites "rated and reviewed" by the McKinley Group, a subsidiary of
   Excite
   URL: http://www.mckinley.com/

4. WebCrawler
   DESCRIPTION: browse "WebCrawler Select Reviews" or search the WWW
   URL: http://WebCrawler.com/

HTTP Indexes

These sites offer searchable indexes or search "engines" (good for locating
specific information).

1. Alta Vista [*recommended*] for its comprehensiveness (see Infoseek
   Guide under HTTP Catalogs/Indexes, above)
   DESCRIPTION: provides a "Simple" and an "Advanced" query, both of
   which offer Web and Usenet searching; see examples of search
   capabilities
   URL: http://altavista.digital.com/

2. HotBot
   DESCRIPTION: this index lets you limit searches by LOCATION
   (CyberPlace, GeoPlace) and MEDIA TYPE (.gif, .txt)
   URL: http://www.hotbot.com/

3. Open Text
   DESCRIPTION: provides a "Power Search" that lets you search using
   multiple fields (Anywhere, Summary, Title, First Heading, URL) and
   multiple logical/Boolean operators (AND, OR, BUTNOT, NEAR, FOLLOWED
   BY)
   URL: http://index.opentext.net/

HTTP Catalogs/Indexes: Multiple Links

These sites offer links to a number of different WWW search tools that may
be searched separately.

1. ALL-IN-ONE Internet Search
   DESCRIPTION: "a compilation of various forms-based search tools found
   on the Internet"
   URL: http://www.albany.net/allinone

2. Beaucoup Search Engines
   DESCRIPTION: "Every Thing Computing"
   URL:http://www.beaucoup.com/engines.html

3. Internet Search Engines
   DESCRIPTION: "a list of the best Internet directories and spiders"
   URL: http://www.internic.net/tools/

4. RiceInfo
   DESCRIPTION: "some of the more useful Internet navigation tools," with
   recommendations
   URL: http://riceinfo.rice.edu/Internet/
5. The Search Page
   DESCRIPTION: "a hotlist for people who want to search the Internet for
   something but don't know where to start"
   URL: http://www.accesscom.com/~ziegler/search.html

6. The Ultimate Internet Search Index
   DESCRIPTION: categories WWW search tools into "General," "Newsgroup,"
   "Business," "Online Shopping," "Email," "Reference," "Regional,"
   "File," "Yellow Page" and "Phone Number"
   URL: http://www.geocities.com/SiliconValley/Heights/5296/

HTTP Indexes: Simultaneous/Integrated Searching

These sites let you search several different search tools at the same time.

1. CYBER 411
   DESCRIPTION: "THE ULTIMATE PARALLEL SEARCH;" the "Fast" feature
   collates search results from different search tools, thus removing
   duplicates
   URL: http://www.cyber411.com/search/

2. MetaCrawler
   DESCRIPTION: a "Parallel Web Search Service" that first sums the
   scores given search results by each search tool and then presents
   these results in "a 'voted' ordering"

URL: http://www.metacrawler.com/

3. ProFusion
DESCRIPTION: "The Best Results from the Best Search Engines, " "Filters
results to remove duplicates "
URL: http://www.designlab.ukans.edu/profusion/

4. SavvySearch
DESCRIPTION: "a meta-search tool;" the "Query option: Integrate
results" collates search results from different search tools , thus
removing duplicates
URL: http://www.cs.colostate.edu/~dreiling/smartform.html

Other HTTP Search Sites

1. The Argus Clearinghouse
DESCRIPTION: full text searching of Internet research guides
URL: http://www.clearinghouse.net/

2. webCATS: Library Catalogs on the World Wide Web
DESCRIPTION: a guide to library catalogs accessible via the WWW (see
HyTelnet under TELNET SEARCH SITES, below)
URL: http://library.usask.ca/hywebcat/

GOPHER SEARCH SITES

1. Netlink Server: Jughead
DESCRIPTION: Subject, Internet tool Type, Geographic and Domain
searching
URL: gopher://honor.uc.wlu.edu:1020/

2. Netlink Server: Veronica
DESCRIPTION: gopherspace and gopher directories searching
URL: gopher://liberty.uc.wlu.edu:70/11/gophers/veronica/

FTP SEARCH SITES

1. Archie Seach Services
DESCRIPTION: WWW Archie search services (gateways)
URL: http://www.lerc.nasa.gov/archieplex/ OR
http://hoohoo.ncsa.uiuc.edu/archie.html

2. clnet's the computer network
DESCRIPTION: "the way to find software on the Internet"
URL: http://www.shareware.com/

3. Tile Net
DESCRIPTION: "A complete reference to Anonymous FTP sites. "
URL: http://tile.net/ftp-list/

TELNET SEARCH SITE

1. HyTelnet
DESCRIPTION: a guide to library catalogs and other information
resources accessible via telnet (see Galaxy, under HTTP

Catalogs/Indexes, above; see also webCATS under Other HTTP Search
Sites, above)
URL: http://library.usask.ca/hytelnet/ OR
http://www.cc.ukans.edu/hytelnet_html/START.TXT.html

NEWS SEARCH SITES
  1. DejaNews
     DESCRIPTION: "The Premier Usenet Search Utility" does not include
     alt.*, soc.* and *.binaries newsgroups
     URL: http://www.dejanews.com/
2. Liszt of Newsgroups
     DESCRIPTION: provides searching of over 15,000 newsgroups
     URL: http://liszt.bluemarble.net/news/

  3. Tile Net
     DESCRIPTION: "The complete reference to Usenet newsgroups."
     URL: http://tile.net/news/

MAILING LIST SEARCH SITES

  1. Directory of Scholarly and Professional E-Conferences
     DESCRIPTION: provides browsing and searching e-conferences
     URL: http://n2h2.com/KOVACS/

  2. Liszt Directory of E-Mail and Discussion Groups
     DESCRIPTION: a database of "listserv, listproc, majordomo and
     independently managed mailing lists"
     URL: http://www.liszt.com/

  3. Tile Net
     DESCRIPTION: "The reference to Internet discussion groups."
     URL: http://tile.net/lists/

WHITE PAGES SEARCH SITE

  1. Netscape Destinations: Whitepages
     DESCRIPTION: "these online white pages provide listings for
     individuals"
     URL: http://home.netscape.com/home/internet-white-pages.html

See also various HTTP indexes, listed above.

BEGINNING OF DOCUMENT

The author of this document (URL = http://libweb.sdsu.edu/gov/search.html)
is Bruce Harley.
E-mail: harley@mail.sdsu.edu

Previous page (THE WORLD WIDE WEB)
  Return to Library Home Page

Last change March 10, 1997.

webmaster@libweb.sdsu.edu

WWW Instruction Evaluation

Date Attended: _____

Department or Major: _____

How did you learn about the WWW instruction?

___Library lobby poster   ___Flyer

___Weekly   ___SDSU WWW Notice

What did you learn from this instruction?
_____

_____

How will you apply what you learned?
_____

_____

What could be eliminated from this instruction?
_____

_____

What could be added to this instruction?
_____

_____

In what ways might the scheduling, content, organization or delivery of this instruction be improved?
_____

_____

Any additional comments?
_____

_____

An Advanced WWW Workshop

BRUCE HARLEY

Associate Librarian, Government Publications & Maps Division
SAN DIEGO STATE UNIVERSITY

CIRCUMSTANCES FOR THE INSTRUCTION SESSION:

See the section on CIRCUMSTANCES FOR THE INSTRUCTION SESSION in the chapter entitled "WWW BASICS; AN INTRODUCTORY WORKSHOP" for a broader historical overview of San Diego State University Library's Internet/WWW instructional program. In 1995, when we first made the WWW the focus of this program, we offered only introductory workshops. As the year progressed and more patrons had either attended an introductory workshop or learned WWW basics elsewhere, the demand for advanced workshops grew.

In 1996, librarians participating in this program began offering different types of advanced workshops. To date, these have included workshops on advanced Netscape techniques, generic and subject-specific (featuring biology, business, government information, Latin American studies, women's studies) searching the Internet workshops and basic HTML workshops.

OBJECTIVES OF THE INSTRUCTION SESSION:

There are several teaching/learning objectives for this advanced WWW workshop. Upon completion of this workshop, attendees should be familiar with:

- the basis for evaluating **networked information search tools**;
- helpful WWW sources of additional information on this topic;
- how to identify different types of search tools, especially WWW (or HTTP) catalogs and indexes;
- how to use different HTTP catalogs and indexes efficiently and effectively; and
- interpreting search results, that is EVALUATING WWW SOURCES OF INFORMATION.

COMPONENTS OF THE LIBRARY INSTRUCTION:

A focus of the advanced WWW workshop is to demonstrate how the WWW can be self-teaching. This is done in part by having the handouts which are listed below accessible via the WWW by all attendees at these workshops:
- "THE WORLD WIDE WEB (WWW)"
- "SEARCH THE WORLD WIDE WEB (WWW)"
- "RECOMMENDED HTTP SEARCH SITES: SEARCH CAPABILITIES"

The URLs for the handouts are, respectively:

- http://libweb.sdsu.edu/gov/wwwdos.html
- http://libweb.sdsu.edu/gov/search.html
- http://libweb.sdsu.edu/gov/recommend.html

Attendees follow librarians' opening lectures by referring to the printed copies of the handouts and also get hands-on experience as part of structured WWW presentations. Text-only versions of the first two handouts are included in this book in the chapter entitled "WWW Basics; An Introductory WWW Workshop." A text-only version of the third handout is included in this chapter.

PART I INTRODUCTION (Lecture/Hands-on Activity; 15 minutes)

During the first 15 minutes, the librarian:
1. introduces him/herself as a librarian and informs attendees where in the Library they can access the WWW;
2. draws attendees' attention to the type of hardware and software they will be using and encourages those familiar with Windows or Macintosh to help their less experienced "networked neighbors";
3. informs attendees that they will be asked to complete an evaluation form at the completion of the workshop;
4. assures attendees that there will be time for questions and answers at the end of the workshop but that it is also OK to ask questions before then; and
5. provides an overview of the contents of the handouts, especially the sections on:
   a. **WWW CHARACTERISTICS—networked information search tools,** and **EVALUATING WWW SOURCES OF INFORMATION** in "THE WORLD WIDE WEB (WWW)" handout,
   b. the opening paragraph and arrangement of the "SEARCH THE WORLD WIDE WEB (WWW)" handout, and
   c. the contents of the "RECOMMENDED HTTP SEARCH SITES: SEARCH CAPABILITIES" handout;
6. covers the section on **WWW CHARACTERISTICS—networked information search tools**, especially the basis for evaluating these tools; and
7. informs attendees of helpful WWW sources of additional information on this topic.

Numbers six and seven are intended as hands-on activities, with attendees connected to the WWW @ http://libweb.sdsu.edu/gov/wwwdos.html#search , the section of "THE World Wide Web (WWW)" on **networked information search tools**.

PART II EVALUATING AND IDENTIFYING DIFFERENT TYPES OF SEARCH TOOLS
Lecture/Hands-On Activity; 20 minutes) [see Activity I in this chapter]

In Part II, attendees apply the basic principles for evaluating **networked information search tools** covered by the librarian in Part I. To do so, they complete Activity I while performing searches using one search tool listed under each of the following types of HTTP SEARCH SITES in "SEARCH THE WORLD WIDE WEB (WWW)" @ http://libweb.sdsu.edu/gov/search.html#http :

1. HTTP Catalog, offering a browsable catalog that organizes WWW resources in broad subject categories (good for locating general information);
2. HTTP Catalogs/Indexes, offering both browsable catalogs that organize WWW resources in broad subject categories (good for locating general information) AND searchable indexes or search "engines" (good for locating specific information);
3. HTTP Catalogs/Indexes and Reviews, offering, in addition to catalogs and indexes, reviews of selected WWW resources;
4. HTTP Indexes, offering searchable indexes or search "engines" (good for locating specific information);
5. HTTP Catalogs/Indexes: Multiple Links, offering links to a number of different WWW search tools that may be searched separately; and
6. HTTP Indexes: Simultaneous/Integrated Searching, offering simultaneous searching of several different search tools at the same time, with or without integrated results.

This activity is intended to help attendees learn:
- how to identify different types of search tools, especially WWW (or HTTP) catalogs and indexes; and
- how to evaluate these search tools.

Non-HTTP search tools (e.g., gopher, FTP, telnet, etc.) may also be included in this activity.

PART III   USING DIFFERENT HTTP CATALOGS AND INDEXES   (Lecture/Hands-On Activity; 30 minutes) [see Activity II in this chapter]

In Part III, attendees compare the detailed search capabilities of the three HTTP SEARCH SITES, linked to and described in "RECOMMENDED HTTP SEARCH SITES: SEARCH CAPABILITIES" @ http://libweb.sdsu.edu/gov/recommend.html :

1. Yahoo, a combined HTTP catalog and index recommended for its catalog;
2. Infoseek (Ultrasmart or Ultraseek), a combined HTTP catalog and index recommended for its search precision; and
3. Alta Vista (Simple), an index recommended for its comprehensiveness.

Completing Activity II is intended to help attendees learn how to use different HTTP catalogs and indexes efficiently and effectively.

PART IV INTERPRETING SEARCH RESULTS/EVALUATING WWW SOURCES OF INFORMATION (Lecture/Hands-On Activity; 15 minutes) [see Activity III in this chapter]

In Part III, attendees learn how to interpret search results, that is, how to evaluate WWW information sources by asking the questions posed in the **EVALUATING WWW SOURCES OF INFORMATION** section of "THE WORLD WIDE WEB (WWW)" @ http://libweb.sdsu.edu/gov/wwwdos.html#evaluating . Attendees are asked to repeat selected searches they performed in Part III in order to complete Activity III.

The three Activities are reviewed at the end of Parts II, III, and IV, respectively. Attendees keep the Activity sheets.

Part V QUESTIONS & ANSWERS/EVALUATION (10 minutes)

The librarian asks for questions and requests that attendees take a few minutes to fill out the "WWW Instruction Evaluation" form. A copy of this form is included in the chapter entitled "WWW Basics; An Introductory Workshop." The librarian also lets attendees know that she or he is available to meet with them individually.

Activity I: Evaluating Networked Information Search Tools

Networked information search tools can be evaluated on the basis of their:
1. scope of coverage (e.g., WWW files only vs. WWW and other files);
2. update frequency;
3. search engine: breadth-first (e.g., top-level WWW documents) vs. depth-first (all WWW documents);
4. search content: titles/headings, brief descriptions, full text, URLs;
5. search capabilities: approximate match, (explicit vs. implicit) logical/Boolean operators, proximity operators, truncation, phrase searching, searchable fields (e.g., title);
6. searchable source features (e.g., location, media type);
7. search speed;
8. search results display: excerpt/keyword-in-context or summary, scoring or ranking (i.e., relevance feedback), URLs, hot links; and
9. help: Frequently Asked Questions (FAQ), search samples, etc.

PERFORM a search of WWW documents using one search tool listed under three of the types of HTTP SEARCH SITES in "SEARCH THE WORLD WIDE WEB (WWW)" @ http://libweb.sdsu.edu/gov/search.html#http .
[See text of handout in the chapter entitled "WWW Basics; An Introductory Workshop"]

RECORD each search tool name and the search terms you entered.

EVALUATE each of the three selected search tools on the basis of the nine criteria listed above. For each criteria, describe what you found to be the strengths or weaknesses of the search tool.

If you were unable to form an opinion on any of the criteria for a search tool, indicate why.

SEARCH TOOL #1: _____
Search terms: _____
1. scope of coverage: _____
2. update frequency: _____
3. search engine: _____
4. search content: _____

5. search capabilities: _____

6. searchable source features: _____

7. search speed: _____

8. search results display: _____

9. help: _____

SEARCH TOOL #2: _____

Search terms: _____

1. scope of coverage: _____

2. update frequency: _____

3. search engine: _____

4. search content: _____

5. search capabilities: _____

6. searchable source features: _____

7. search speed: _____

8. search results display: _____

9. help: _____

SEARCH TOOL #3: _____

Search terms: _____

1. scope of coverage: _____

2. update frequency: _____

3. search engine: _____

4. search content: _____

5. search capabilities: _____

6. searchable source features: _____

7. search speed: _____

8. search results display: _____

9. help: _____

Student..

Activity II: Search Capabilities of HTTP Search Sites

The detailed search capabilities of three recommended HTTP SEARCH SITES are outlined below:

1. **Yahoo, a combined HTTP catalog and index recommended for its catalog**
zen buddhism = zen and buddhism (The default search can be duplicated by either:
   +zen +buddhism OR
   zen AND buddhism, available on the SEARCH OPTIONS page only.)
zen OR buddhism = zen or buddhism (Available on the SEARCH OPTIONS page only.)
zen -buddhism = zen but not buddhism
zen buddh* = zen and buddha, buddhists, buddhism, etc.
zen wom*n = zen and (woman or women)
"zen buddhism" = zen buddhism
t:zen = zen in WWW document titles only
url:zen = zen in URLs only

2. **Infoseek, a combined HTTP catalog & index recommended for its search precision**
zen buddhism = zen or buddhism
+zen +buddhism = zen and buddhism
zen -buddhism = zen but not buddhism
"zen buddhism" = zen buddhism
title:zen = zen in WWW document titles only
url:zen = zen in URLs only
site:zen.org = zen.org in WWW site names only

3. **Alta Vista (Simple), an index ecommended for its comprehensiveness.**
zen buddhism = zen or buddhism
+zen +buddhism = zen and buddhism
zen -buddhism = zen but not buddhism
zen buddh* = zen and buddha, buddhists, buddhism, etc.
zen wom*n = zen and (woman or women)
"zen buddhism" = zen buddhism
title:zen = zen in WWW document titles only
url:zen = zen in URLs only
host:zen = zen in WWW server host names only

All three HTTP SEARCH SITES are linked to from "RECOMMENDED HTTP SEARCH SITES: SEARCH CAPABILITIES" @ http://libweb.sdsu.edu/gov/recommend.html. [See text of handout in this chapter] Use **Yahoo, Infoseek** and **Alta Vista (Simple)** to search for WWW documents with the words zen and buddhism:

1. anywhere in the text of the documents;
2. anywhere in the text of the documents, but used as a phrase
3. in the titles of the documents.

Record how you entered each search and the number of search results you retrieved.

SEARCH #1:   zen and buddhism anywhere in the text of the documents
1A. Yahoo Search: _____
1B. Yahoo Results: _____
2A. Infoseek Search: _____
2B. Infoseek Results: _____
3A. Alta Vista Search: _____
3B. Alta Vista Results: _____

SEARCH #2:   zen and buddhism anywhere in the text of the documents, but used as
              a phrase
1A. Yahoo Search: _____
1B. Yahoo Results: _____
2A. Infoseek Search: _____
2B. Infoseek Results: _____
3A. Alta Vista Search: _____
3B. Alta Vista Results: _____

SEARCH #3:   zen and buddhism in the titles of the documents
1A. Yahoo Search: _____
1B. Yahoo Results: _____
2A. Infoseek Search: _____
2B. Infoseek Results: _____
3A. Alta Vista Search: _____
3B. Alta Vista Results: _____

PLEASE NOTE:
1. A search submitted in **Yahoo** that retrieves no matching Yahoo Categories or Yahoo Sites, will automatically be performed using **Alta Vista**.
2. **Alta Vista** also offers an **Advanced** query mode and features **LiveTopics**. You are encouraged to explore these after you have become familiar with the **Simple** query mode.

Activity III: Interpreting Search Results

The following questions should be asked when INTERPRETING SEARCH RESULTS, that is, evaluating WWW information sources:

1. Who is responsible for publishing the information provided by the source? What are the credentials and affiliation or sponsorship of any named individuals or organizations? How authoritative are they?

2. What can be said about the content, context, style, structure, completeness and accuracy of the information provided by the source? Are any conclusions offered? If so, based on what criteria and supported by what secondary and primary documentation?

3. When was the information provided by the source published? Is the information provided by the source in its original form or has it been revised? Is this information updated regularly?

4. Where else can the information provided by the source be found on the WWW? Is this information authentic? Is this information unique or has it been copied?

5. Why was the information provided by the source published? What are the perspectives, opinions, assumptions and biases of whomever is responsible for this information? Who is the intended audience?

Repeat any three of the searches you performed in the previous exercise (see Activity II). Record the URL for the first search result listed for each search. Select a different search result listing if necessary to avoid duplication. Answer as many of the questions listed above as possible for each of the three search results.

SEARCH RESULT #1:   _____
1. Who?   _____
2. What?   _____
3. When?   _____
4. Where?   _____
5. Why?   _____

SEARCH RESULT #2: _____
1. Who? _____
2. What? _____
3. When? _____
4. Where? _____
5. Why? _____

SEARCH RESULT #3: _____
1. Who? _____
2. What? _____
3. When? _____
4. Where? _____
5. Why? _____

[Malcolm A. Love Library]

RECOMMENDED HTTP SEARCH SITES: SEARCH CAPABILITIES

Here are examples of the search capabilities of the recommended HTTP search sites.

Yahoo, a combined HTTP catalog and index recommended for its catalog @ http://www.yahoo.com/.

* zen buddhism = zen and buddhism (The default search can be duplicated
  by either:
    o +zen +buddhism OR
    o zen AND buddhism, available on the SEARCH OPTIONS page only)
* zen OR buddhism = zen or buddhism (Available on the SEARCH OPTIONS
  page only.)
* zen -buddhism = zen but not buddhism
* zen buddh* = zen and buddha, buddhists, buddhism, etc.
* zen wom*n = zen and (woman or women)
* "zen buddhism" = zen buddhism
* t:zen = zen in WWW document titles only
* url:zen = zen in URLs only

Your search results "will be a list of matching Yahoo Categories followed by a list of matching Yahoo Sites. If no matching Yahoo Categories and Sites are found, Yahoo will automatically perform a Web-wide, full-text document search using the Alta Vista search engine" (see below).

Infoseek (Ultrasmart or Ultraseek), a combined HTTP catalog and index recommended for its search precision @ http://guide.infoseek.com/.

* zen buddhism = zen or buddhism
* +zen +buddhism = zen and buddhism
* zen -buddhism = zen but not buddhism
* "zen buddhism" = zen buddhism
* title:zen = zen in WWW document titles only
* url:zen = zen in URLs only
* site:zen.org = zen.org in WWW site names only

Alta Vista, recommended for its comprehensiveness.

* Simple, an HTTP index @ http://altavista.digital.com/.
    o zen buddhism = zen or buddhism
    o +zen +buddhism = zen and buddhism
    o zen -buddhism = zen but not buddhism
    o zen buddh* = zen and buddha, buddhists, buddhism, etc.
    o zen wom*n = zen and (woman or women)
    o "zen buddhism" = zen buddhism
    o title:zen = zen in WWW document titles only

o url:zen = zen in URLs only
o host:zen = zen in WWW server host names only

* Advanced, an HTTP index @
  http://altavista.digital.com/cgi=bin/query?pg=aq.
  o zen AND buddhism = zen and buddhism
  o zen OR buddhism = zen or buddhism
  o zen AND NOT buddhism = zen but not buddhism
  o zen NEAR buddhism = zen within 10 words of buddhism

The Advanced search capabilities are intended to be used with the "Results Ranking Criteria" feature which lets you "enter words or phrases that will determine the ranking of the search results."

Alta Vista features LiveTopics, " a tool that helps you refine and analyze search results. Read all about it "@
http://altavista.digital.com/av/lt/help.html.

The author of this document URL=http://libweb.sdsu.edu/gov/recommend.html is Bruce Harley.
Email: harley@mail.sdsu.edu

Previous page (SEARCH THE WORLD WIDE WEB)

  Return to Library Home Page

Last change February 19, 1997

webmaster@libweb.sdsu.edu

ACRES: Accessibility, Content, Relevance, Effectiveness and Stability of Internet Sites

NECIA PARKER-GIBSON
Library Instruction Coordinator
UNIVERSITY OF ARKANSAS, FAYETTEVILLE

Circumstances for the Instruction Session:

The acronym ACRES stands for:
>   A=accessibility,
>   C=content,
>   R=relevance,
>   E=effectiveness, and
>   S=stability of Internet sites.

The basic ACRES handout (which is included in this chapter) has been used in library instruction classes in several ways which I will briefly describe in the paragraphs which follow.

One instance was a class of freshmen students in social sciences, whose instructor was eager to have the students exposed to evaluation of all types of sources. We used three full class sessions to cover the library catalog and some of the reasons academic libraries hold what they do, evaluation of printed sources, as well as evaluation of Internet sources.

Another use of ACRES was to provide tips or guidance for upper level journalism classes in editing and reporting when the professors were intent on getting the students to use sources which could be accessed from their workstations.

Plus, a speech class where the instructor encouraged the use of Internet sources heavily or exclusively, provided a further opportunity to teach ACRES. I have also used the handout on its own as a way of covering the subject without lecturing on it, because the students expressed interest in the concepts covered but there wasn't time for any in-depth discussion.

Objectives of the Instruction:

- Students will be able to identify domain sources, at least preliminarily, as educational, nonprofit or commercial (i.e., by .edu, .org, .com, and by content and structure).
- Students will be able to recognize and state that site providers and content vary in quality as much as or more than printed sources.

- Students will be able to state why sites whose providers and authors are identified are more authoritative than sites that do not show these parameters.
- Students will be made aware that search engines cover different areas or subsets of the Internet.

Components of the Instruction:

TEACHING EVALUATION OF INTERNET/WWW SOURCES. The Internet is a source of varied and often useful information. But many who use it are being overwhelmed, or even drowned, by the sheer quantity of Internet sites. While many sites perform their particular function admirably, sorting out the bad sites can be challenging. Let's not forget that many library users have been, and possibly still are, overwhelmed by libraries and their complexities.

Some factors to consider when evaluating sources on the Internet are accessibility, content and design. Although review sites that award points to the best web pages and sites are becoming common, and software that sift through sites to find the top ones according to chosen criteria are becoming available, most users must still apply their own judgment. Guidelines are helpful to many, especially in public, professional or academic situations where they are being asked to use Internet sources as references for other work. I suggest evaluation parameters (see also McClements and Becker)for Internet sites that are similar to those used for evaluation of printed (Katz, and others) or computerized sources, and some additional points which are unique to the Net. Not all points will need to be considered in every case, since much use of Internet sites is informal. The elements below are some major considerations, tagged by the acronym ACRES:

A=Accessibility

How easy is it to get to the site?
How accessible is the site? Levels of connectivity to the Internet still vary greatly due to hardware, software, and connection cost considerations. (Lane and Summerhill) While Monica Brinkley and Mary Burke have rated the various Internet search *tools* (Alta Vista, Lycos, Gophers, et. al.) for ease of use, type of searching available and other parameters, including menus and help screens, you should consider the overall availability of a given site across software thresholds or platforms.

Sites vary, from the most simple directory software, which is command and menu-driven, to the most elaborate combinations of text, graphics, and other media. Some sites are sources of documents or files to be transmitted to your computer, which may or may not have the capability to accept the files (Venditto); many FTP sites (i.e., Project Gutenburg) fall in this category. Although, with the growth of the World Wide Web (WWW), the trend is to put the material on servers for screen access, with downloading or printing becoming secondary, software and hardware capability still varies from individual to individual. Even the theoretically best sites are of no use to those who cannot access them.

Can the site be read by the common text browsers, such as *lynx*? Can it be read by common graphical browsers, including *Internet Explorer* or *Netscape*? Is it intelligible or useful only by graphical browser? Many sites, including some of the search engines, have screens that are **not intuitive** to new users when used by text browser. For example, if you try one of the commercial phone directories (at http://www.bigyellow.com) with *lynx*, a text browser, as opposed to a graphical interface, in the text interface, very little is obvious.

If one compares the estimated number of users of the Internet to the number of the copies of software sold or given away, many Internet users are still working with text browsers, despite the excitement over graphical browsers. The easiest way to demonstrate this problem to students is to project a well-designed site, and then contrast it with a poorly-designed counterpart, in the same subject area, or even the same site, such as Big Yellow's page, much more facile under a graphical browser, vs. their page as a text version.

How easy is it to use the site?
Is the material on the screen when you open the location? Sites which require students to dig through many menus or levels to get to the information are not the best choice. Usability studies recommend no more than two levels of menu between the user and the main source of information. (Schneiderman, 1992) Pages that are indexed by an internal search engine, with the entire document searched, rather than only a screen's worth at one time, are a better bet. Most browsers have some search capability built in, but not all sites allow it.

How easy is it to find the site?
Where is the site listed or indexed? Can it be found by keyword searching using most of the available search engines, such as Lycos, InfoSeek, Harvest, et al.? Like GUI (graphical user interface, i.e., Windows, Mac OS) menu titles, the keywords in the site titles should be common enough to be thought of by most users in relation to the subject (Wiklund, 1994), but sufficiently unique to reduce false drops or partial matches, which may swamp the students.

Agenda/Purpose
What is the site's purpose? Why is the information being provided? Some of the Internet sites are the virtual equivalent of the "I married an alien" press, or examples of vanity press (Tillman) while others are devoted to serious information dispersal or research support. Many students don't realize that the domain name endings: .edu, .org, or .com, provide some clues to the providers' intention, although not always a seal of approval on content.

The purpose of an educational site should be to provide unique information, such as the National Gallery of Art site or various library catalogs. Remind the students to consider whether a database, an encyclopedia, or other reference work might be available locally or in a more recent version. Most online copies of *Roget's Thesaurus* are the 1911 edition, which has new printed editions listed in Books in Print for 1996, or don't list publication data at all, and most searchable copies of *Familiar Quotations (Bartlett's)*, such as the site at Columbia University, are the 1901 edition, because of copyright limitations. The most recent edition in our library, by contrast, is the sixteenth edition, published in 1992.

Is the purpose of the site to provide social interaction? Entertainment? Personal information? If the site is designed to provide profit to the organizers, it may be cheaper to find another site or another venue.

Is the purpose of the site to advertise products or services, such as the many catalogs online? Is there enough additional information to make it a *value-added* site? Some sites are focused solely on selling a product; others are using the Web to educate consumers or support research, as a service. An example of the latter is the homepage of *Ben and Jerry's Homemade, Inc.*, which provides research information such as current annual reports, bibliographies about the company, and other material, such as crafts for children and humor.

Students should consider the site's agenda(s), remembering that they may not always be obvious. What are the publishers' biases? Certainly, the home pages of some groups of white supremacists make their position known early and often, but many pages are not so transparent. If students are depending on a site for more than its entertainment value, it is important, perhaps imperative, to know the background and intentions of the publishers.

Authority
The authority of the writers and providers of a site is a related issue to purpose and agenda. Who is providing the information? Authors and designers should be willing to identify themselves with their work, and providers, if different, should also identify themselves. There is some desire for confidentiality for security reasons since anyone can read what is online, but there should be at least one contact point or E-mail address. (Lemay) What are the credentials of the authors or providers? Are they listed in the text? Available by source code? Do the authors identify their sources? Citation of sources is still both courteous and necessary to avoid plagiarism. Is there a particular reason that this institution or individual provides this page? Is there a historical, professional or personal reason? (Tillman)

C=Content

Content
Is the content accurate? Is the information of sufficient depth or breadth to make access worthwhile? The needs of the user determine utility, but some sites are obvious fluff. Are there additional links that lead to related material? Are the additional links purposeful and meaningful? How easy is it to return from a followed link? (Lemay) Do the images, if any, contribute to the use of the document? Is the document so full of graphics that it takes more than 15 seconds to load (see Response Time)? Is the best use possible only over time (requiring multiple uses)?

Cost and Other Considerations

Is the site free? Does it require a subscription? A one-time fee? Does it require registration as a user, including E-mail addresses? After registration at a site, do you then receive unsolicited E-mail? Some entertainment sites, such as MUDD sites or chat lines, can cost an individual or institution huge amounts of connect and system time, without showing concrete benefit to the individuals involved. It is very easy to run up bills of hundreds of dollars a year accessing these things through commercial vendors, given connect time and charges per minute, and there are other costs, including opportunity costs, both social and financial. I suggest to students that the Internet can be a time-eater as well as a time-saver.

Currency

Is the information timely as well as accurate? Is the material updated as needed? Some material is timeless, such as art, but other material is ephemeral; the saying "yesterday's paper wraps today's fish" may apply to sites with time-sensitive material if it is not updated. In addition, a site with yesterday's newspaper but not last week's or last month's, offers limited utility to the users. The lack of archives on the Internet is one of its flaws for research purposes.

R=Relevance

Relevance

Is the material appropriate for the query, research, or entertainment of the users? How good is the information? How is the quality of the graphics? Is the site or the information worth accessing in the first place? Is there enough depth to the information? Most sites do not include background material or definitions of terms.

Response Time

How long does it take for an Internet site to be loaded? While this is variable, and partially machine-related, a response time of 15 seconds is considered to be the upper limit of most users' patience (Schneiderman, 1992), although variation within that time (1-15 seconds) is not a cause for much anxiety among users. A courteous designer will allow users to choose to load the pages without the images (text only) to speed loading (Lemay) or to accommodate text browsers. Does loading without images prevent full understanding of the document? For example, one local newspaper site uses images as button links, but does not provide word cues, so that if the site is viewed via a text browser, the only way to choose links to other parts of the newspaper file is by trial and error.

Does the elapsed time to load a document vary by the time of day? Does high use keep a particular site from loading at certain times of day? Response time is not under the full control of the designers, but a good page will on average be built to load in a few seconds on most client/servers.

E=Effectiveness

Arrangement

Is the site easy to use? Are the buttons or links logical and consistent? Are the screens well- organized and easy to read? Are the screens cluttered?

Design of screens is more difficult in the Internet environment, because of its free-form nature. Unlike most interfaces, such as those used for software (Schneiderman, 1992, Crawford, 1992), the programs or documents are not necessarily being accessed specifically in order to do a set of routine tasks, as with a word processing program, to search an online catalog or other database, or to learn a circumscribed body of material or to use for training or testing as with computer-assisted instruction. How a site is manipulated is far more user-driven than for most software, although the type of software, the purposes and the content of the documents will determine their usage. Because the nature of Internet searching is to bounce from site to site, there is less chance to develop key stroke or memory "macros," and the result is often frustration or confusion, since what works at one site may not work at another. The lack of common commands or command languages is partly offset by the ability to point and click, in the graphical browsers, or to use the arrow keys in most text browsers.

The most important arrangement issue is whether the design of the screen helps or hinders work. One effect of the rise of graphical browsers on the Internet is to make every page a graphical user interface, so similar design rules (Crawford, 1992, McDonald, et al, 1991, Fowler, 1995, Wiklund, 1994), as have been used for screen design in software programs and online catalog screens, still apply. Simplicity, consistency, and legibility are key attributes.

Desk-top publishing studies show that people continue to read left to right, and from the top, diagonally (Metz and Junion-Metz, 1994), so the most important elements should be at the head, on the left, and buttons or other activators are most likely to be noticed on the lower right corner of the screen. Many common design problems involving clarity and continuity remain, although many sites can be seen to improve over time, sometimes almost overnight.

Is there any provision made for the sight-impaired or hearing-impaired, either in the number and types of keystrokes or mouse clicks required to operate a site, or if much of the content involves graphical elements or sound? (Grassian) As hardware and software improvements, with resultant ease of use, allow more ADA access and as more of the population in general comes online, this becomes a consideration. As the population of users ages, this will become more of an issue.

Style

Is the text or content focused on the needs of the users? Are the sentences and directions clear? Is the grammar correct? What about the spelling? Is the use of all CAPITALS limited to warnings or other points that need emphasis? (Schneiderman) Do the pages or screens show their relation to each other by common design elements or labeling? Laura Lemay suggests that each page or screen should be self-sufficient in the hypertext environment because one never knows if individuals will follow the sequence of screens one had in mind during the design period.

Is the material edited from time to time, adding new or more current information or features as software changes, or does it look dated? Is it interactive, using buttons, forms and feedback? If so, do the added features work coherently? Are forms self-explanatory? Can you find the related buttons or other tools easily? Directions must be simple in software environments which usually do not include context-specific online help, and where the circumstances of use are hard to forecast.

The format or layout of an Internet or Web page is dependent on the client (computer and software) that is reading the document, and is not in the complete control of the server (computer that is home to the files). Have the authors done what they can to ensure clarity? Is the mixture of fonts or styles (i.e., bolding, italics) logical and consistent? Is it easy to pick out the links, if any? Are the link tags descriptive of the content, rather than the words "click," "link" or "here"? (Lemay) Does the layout of the page, the background, or the wallpaper, make text difficult to read, or does it interfere with images or buttons? Even the best information is hard to find and use on badly designed screens or databases.

S=Stability

Stability

Is the site stable? Does the link address change frequently? If the address changes, a new link should be made, and a page left open with the new address or link listed. If the author or sponsor of a site changes, that should be made public too. Sites that disappear without a forwarding address are frustrating to all, and acknowledgment of changes in author, editor or sponsor is simply good manners. Commercial and institutional sites seem to be more stable at present than personal or social sites, for reasons of financial and staff support.

Conclusion

The result of these considerations is this: a streamlined, simple, accurate and accessible site which is inexpensive or free and which gives the users the information desired is obviously the best value. Graphics, sound and video clips, and all the other software and hardware intensive possibilities will become useful only as they become faster, cheaper and more universally readable across platforms, and if the content of the site is worthwhile from the start.

Internet site evaluation by "ACRES"

A=Accessibility
C=Content
R=Relevance
E=Effectiveness
S=Stability of Internet Sites

Traditional measures used to evaluate books
and other materials can be adapted to Internet sources,
however, consider the additional criteria which are
outlined below.

<u>A</u>CRES = access, agenda, arrangement, authority

Accessibility

How easy is it to get to the site? Can it be read by many kinds of software?
How easy is it to use the site? Are the screens logical and the directions clear?
How do you find it? Is it listed or indexed by common Internet search engines?

Agenda, Audience, and Purpose

What is the site's agenda or purpose? Why is the information being provided?
Educational sites (.edu) should provide unique information, such as the National
Gallery of Art site or various library catalogs.

Nonprofit sites (.org) may provide a variety of materials. The Public
Broadcasting site, at www.pbs.org, is an example.

Commercial sites (.com) will advertise products or services, such as the many
catalogs online. Is there enough additional information to make it a value-added
site? For example, some firms include information about the company such as
annual reports, or do-it-yourself tips. Social sites may or may not be worth the
cost.

Arrangement

Is the site easy to use? Are the buttons or links logical and consistent? Are the
screens easy to read?

Authority

Who is providing the information? Authors and/or providers should be willing to
identify themselves with their work, and designers, if different, should also
identify themselves. What are the providers' credentials? Are they experts in
their field? Do they tell you?

ACRES = content, cost, currency

Content

Is the content accurate? Is it of sufficient depth or breadth to make access worthwhile? Are there additional links that lead to related material? Are the links to other material logical and meaningful? Do the links work? Is it easy to get back?

Cost

Is the site free? Does it require a subscription or a fee? Does it require registration, including an E-mail address? After you register at a site, do you then receive unsolicited E-mail or regular mail?

Currency

Is the information timely as well as accurate? Is the material updated as needed?

ACRES = relevance, response time

Relevance

Does the material address your question, research or entertainment needs? How good is the information? Is it worth accessing in the first place?

Response Time

How long does it take to load? Does the site allow users to choose to load the pages without the images (text only) to speed loading or accommodate text browsers? Does the loss or removal of graphics interfere with meaning? Does the elapsed time to access or load a document vary by the time of day? Response time is not under the full control of the designers, but a good page will be built to load in a few seconds on most clients, on average.

ACRES = efficient use of time, effort, equipment

Effective use of time

If you use a site, is it a good use of your time? Is there a better way to find the information you need?

Efficient use of the effort, energy, and equipment?

As a source of information, does the site provide enough to make it the best use of effort and equipment?

ACRES = stability, style

Stability

Is the site stable? Does the link address change frequently? Is a page left open with the new address or link?

Style

Is the text or content focused on your needs? Are the sentences and directions clear? Are the grammar and spelling correct? Is the use of all CAPITALS limited to warnings or other points that need emphasis?

Do the pages or screens show their relation to each other, by common design elements, labeling or directional cues? Is it interactive, using buttons, forms and feedback? If so, do the added features work coherently? Do they add to the utility of the page?

Necia Parker-Gibson, 5/96

References:

Brinkley, Monica and Mary Burke. "Information Retrieval From the Internet: an Evaluation of the Tools." *Internet Research: Electronic Networking Applications and Policy* 5, no.3 (1995): 3-10.

Crawford, Walt. "Starting Over: Current Issues in Online Catalog User Interface Design." *Information Technology and Libraries* 11 (March 1992): 62-76.

Grassian, Esther. "Thinking Critically About World Wide Web Resources." (July 21, 1995). In Nahl, Diane. *Psychology of Homepage Architecture.* via lynx at http://www2.hawaii.edu/slis/nahl/nahl.html on March 8, 1996.

Katz, William. *Introduction to Reference Work: Basic Information Sources.* New York: McGraw-Hill Publishing Co., 1974, 19-20.

Lane, Elisabeth and Craig Summerhill. *Internet Primer for Information Professionals: a Basis Guide to Internet Networking Technology.* Westport, CT: Meckler, 1993.

Lemay, Laura. *Teach Yourself Web Publishing with HTML in a Week.* Indianapolis, Ind.: Sams Publishing, 1995.

McClements, Nancy and Cheryl Becker. "Writing Web Page Standards." *College and Research Libraries News* 57 (January 1996): 16-17.

MacDonald, Linda Brew, et al. *Teaching Technologies in Libraries : a Practical Guide.* Boston, Mass. : G.K. Hall, 1990.

Metz, Ray E. and Gail Junion-Metz. "Using DTP and Graphic Design to Improve Library Publications." Presentation. Walt Crawford, moderator. Miami Beach: American Library Association Annual Conference, June 26, 1994.

Schneiderman, Ben. *Designing the User Interface: Strategies for Effective Human-Computer Interaction.* 2nd edition. Reading, Mass.: Addison-Wesley Publishing Co., 1992.

Tillman, Hope N. "Evaluating Quality on the Net." February 26, 1996. Via Netscape 2.0 at http://www.tiac.net/users/hope/findqual.html on May 8, 1996.

Venditto, Gus. "Online Services: How Does Their Internet Access Stack Up?" *Internet World*, 7 (March 1996) 55-65.

Wiklund, Michael E., ed. *Usability in Practice: How Companies Develop User-Friendly Products.* Boston: AP Professional, 1994.

Notes:

Biographical Information on the Internet; A Web Tutorial

BARBARA L. CRESSMAN

Visiting Reference Instruction Coordinator & Assistant Professor
UNIVERSITY OF ILLINOIS, URBANA-CHAMPAIGN

Circumstances for the Instruction Session:

A major component of unmasking the Internet for research is deciding when the Internet is a good, and possibly the best, choice for finding certain types of information. Just as in more traditional sources, the Internet has its strengths and weakness as a format for reference resources.

The Web-based interactive tutorial introduced in this chapter was developed for the University of Illinois Library, Urbana-Champaign (UIUC). It provides students with the skills needed to use both print and electronic resources. The instructional modules orient the user to the unique UIUC reference collection while teaching evaluation skills for Internet and networked resources. This tutorial can be accessed at http://surya.grainger.uiuc.edu/rex/instruction/biog.htm.

Announcement of this lesson is made through several channels:
- the "What's New icon on the top level reference home page;
- handouts of currently available user education;
- course-integrated library instruction, especially literature and history classes; and
- notices in the campus newspapers.

Biographical Information is one of a set of modules designed to guide the user through a series of critical thinking exercises on choosing the most appropriate reference resources for the particular need. Each module encourages the student to identify selection criteria and learn evaluation skills by becoming acquainted with the features of the selected reference resources. Knowing how to find and evaluate the best information sources provides the student with the cognitive tools to make informed decisions throughout the research process. These tools include valuable information seeking skills which will be useful over a lifetime.

Objectives of the Instruction:

- To increase awareness that information on the Web is easily accessible—but in most cases should be combined with information from print resources to insure thorough research of biographical materials.
- To help students make informed decisions about choosing the most appropriate reference resources through learned skills in critical evaluation of resources.

- To provide examples of resources with descriptive information to be examined in the process of selection and evaluation—techniques for evaluating print resources can be used for Web resources as well.

Components of the Instruction:

PART 1 LOCATING THE BIOGRAPHY RESOURCES:
- Links to the resource examples as well as additional biography resources.
- Links to subject directories and search engines useful for finding biography resources.
- Call numbers of print resources located in the UIUC Reference Library.

PART 2 IDENTIFYING SELECTION CRITERIA:
- How do I want to be able to search for this information?
- How is the information in this resource arranged and what are the access points?
- How much information do I want? Do I want only the answer to my question, or would I like additional related information as well?

PART 3 EVALUATING THE RESOURCES:
The questions which follow are basic questions which a user must ask about information found on the Internet.

What is the intended audience?
> Is this resource intended for scholarly research? Internet users beware, you may follow a link to what looks to be a great resource, only to find it is basically a vanity page used to air personal views and opinions. Web standards to ensure accuracy are yet to be developed.

What is the coverage of the biography resource?
> What is the coverage? In general, biographical resources on the Internet do not have the depth of coverage of print resources, and it is often difficult to determine the extent of coverage of a Web resource.

How current is it?
> How often is this resource updated? Dates are not always included on Web pages. If the date is included, it may indicate when first written, when placed on the Web, or when last revised.

PART 4 BECOMING ACQUAINTED WITH BASIC FEATURES OF RESOURCES:
Selected resources for biographical information are listed in the section which follows. The resources are grouped under three categories: (1) General Biography; (2) National Biography, and (3) Biographies of Professionals in Selected Fields. All of these resources can be found either in paper format in the UIUC Reference Library or accessed through the Internet. In the Web-based tutorial of this instruction module, these resources appear in a table which gives brief information about the arrangement and coverage of each. See the table at the end of the chapter.

General Biography

A&E Television Network Biography Database*
Biographical Dictionary: Notable Citizens of the Planet*
Biography and Genealogy Master Index
Biography Index
Current Biography
Newspaper Abstracts (especially obituaries)**
> Sometimes a personal name search on the Internet will retrieve biographical information (not very reliable.)

National Biography

American Biographical Archive
American Men and Women of Science
Dictionary of American Biography
National Cyclopedia of American Biography
Who was Who in America
Who's Who in America

Biographies of Professionals in Selected Fields

Anthology of Middle English Literature*
Biographies of Saints and Thoughts on Hinduism*
Business and Economy: Biographies*
Classic TV Biographies - Cast Member Biography*
Contemporary Authors
De Imperatoribus Romanis: An Online Encyclopedia of Roman Emperors*
Directory of American Scholars
Entertainment: Actors and Actresses*
Eric's Treasure Trove of Scientific Biography*
European Faculty Directory
Faculty White Pages
NASA Astronaut Biographies*
National Faculty Directory
Politics in America
Presidents of the United States: POTUS*
Primatologist Biographies*
Sixteenth Century Renaissance English Literature*
The Almanac of American Politics
USA Gymnastics Official Biography Index*
Women Mathematicians*

*   Indicates this resource is found on the Internet
**   Indicates this resource is available through FirstSearch

PART 5 EXERCISES IN CHOOSING THE MOST APPROPRIATE BIOGRAPHICAL RESOURCES.

The exercises in the interactive Web-based module are displayed in frames format, and the student answers questions from one frame by selecting titles of resources from another frame. When the selected resource is not the most appropriate choice, the student has the option to link back to review selection criteria, evaluation criteria, and the list of resources accompanied by access/coverage information.

Evaluation:

The success of this project will be measured and evaluated in two ways:

1. Because the exercises are interactive, the learning progress of the user is self-evaluated. The exercises will be displayed in frames format, and the user will answer questions from one frame by selecting titles of resources from another frame. When the selected resource is not the most appropriate choice, the user has the option to link back to review selection criteria, evaluation criteria, and the list of resources accompanied by access/coverage information.

1. An electronic fill-in form will appear at the bottom of the instruction module. This form will give the user the opportunity to once again self-evaluate, as well as provide useful feedback to the developer of the project.

Biography Resources

* Indicates the resource is found on the Internet

GENERAL BIOGRAPHY	ARRANGEMENT & AVAILABILITY	COVERAGE
A&E Television Network Biography Database*	Searchable database.	15,000 entries for celebrities, entertainers, politicians, and many other people, both past and present.
Biographical Dictionary: Notable Citizens of the Planet	Searchable. Includes ideas on how to find biographical information in specific subject areas.	Biographical information on over 15,000 people from ancient times to the present.
Biography and Genealogy Master Index	On CD-ROM and in print format.	Comprehensive index to biographical reference tools during specified time periods.
Biography Index	Print format.	Contains citations to biographical articles in scholarly and popular journals, and to biographical essays or chapters in collected biographical books.
Current Biography	Print format.	Published monthly and cumulated in an annual volume. Lengthy essays on "people in the news." Includes obituary notices for individuals who have been the subject of earlier *Current Biography* essays.
Newspaper Abstracts (especially obituaries)	*FirstSearch* database	*FirstSearch* database indexes and abstracts over 25 national and regional newspapers while CD-ROM database is limited to 8 major newspapers. Coverage is from 1989 the present.

NATIONAL BIOGRAPHY	ARRANGEMENT; AVAILABILITY	COVERAGE
American Biographical Archive	Print format.	This source offers reproduced biographical profiles of Americans from biographical reference works of the nineteenth and early twentieth centuries. It should be consulted when an individual is not listed in the printed retrospective sets for deceased Americans.
American Men and Women of Science	Print format.	Biographical information on scientists.
Dictionary of American Biography	Print format.	Covers people who have contributed in a significant way to American political, social, or cultural life.
National Cyclopedia of American Biography	Print format. Consult index as entries are not listed in alphabetical order.	More individuals covered than *Dictionary of American Biography* but not as scholarly.
Who's Who in America	Print format.	Revised every other year, source devotes one paragraph to each person covered. Inclusion varies. Information includes birth date, career accomplishments, education, address, and some other personal information. See also *Who Was Who in America* and regional Who's Who editions.
Who Was Who in America	Print format.	Similar to *Who's Who* but exclusive to figures no longer living.

BIOGRAPHIES OF PROFESSIONALS IN SELECTED FIELDS	ARRANGEMENT; AVAILABILITY	COVERAGE
Anthology of Middle English Literature*	Arranged in sections by author and by subject.	Biographical material and representative works from Chaucer, Langland, Julian of Norwich, Kempe, Malory, and others.
Classic TV Biographies - Cast Member Biography*	Alphabetical order.	Actresses and actors from the period 1956-1965

Table continues on next page

Contemporary Authors	On CD-ROM and in print format.	Very comprehensive source for writers. It lists published works of authors, contains interviews and other information. The index contains references to other Gale literary reference tools.
De Imperatoribus Romanis: An Online Encyclopedia of Roman Emperors*	Alphabetical and chronological.	Biographical essays of the Roman emperors from the accession of the Emperor Augustus to the death of the Emperor Constantine XI Palaeologus.
Directory of American Scholars	Print format.	Information similar to that available in Who's Who but restricted to scholars in history, law, languages, philosophy, religion, and other areas of humanities.
Eric's Treasure Trove of Scientific Biography*	Alphabetical order within frames but you may select the no frames version.	Biographies of figures in the general sciences.
European Faculty Directory	Print format. Alphabetical and subject-oriented listings.	Faculty in Eastern and Western Europe.
NASA Astronaut Biographies*	Searchable. Names in alphabetical order within categories.	Astronauts, astronaut candidates, shuttle crew.
National Faculty Directory	Print format.	Office addresses (no phone) for faculty members at American and some Canadian institutions.
Politics in America	Print format.	Essays on the personal and political lives of U.S. Senators and Representatives. Brief entries for governors plus political information on states and congressional districts.
Presidents of the United States: POTUS*	Presidents in chronological order. Subject and name indexes covering broad range subjects and people related to the Presidency.	Background information, election results, cabinet members, and esoteric information.
Sixteenth Century Renaissance English Literature*	Chronological order.	Biographical information and representative works from Sir Thomas More to Aemilia Lanyer
The Almanac of American Politics	Searchable by state, name, and Senate and House committees. Also in print format.	Contains a wealth of information on Congressmen and the constituencies they represent.
USA Gymnastics Official Biography Index*	Alphabetical order in three categories: women, men, and rhythmic gymnasts.	Limited to U.S. athletes.
Women Mathematicians*	Names in both alphabetical and chronological order.	Limited number but good depth of those covered.

Notes:

Biographical Sources ; Or, How to Write an Obituary

MARILYN P. WHITMORE
Editor
LIBRARY INSTRUCTION PUBLICATIONS

Circumstances for the Instruction Session:

One assignment in Newspaper I (journalism class) at the University of Pittsburgh requires that the students write an obituary of a person who is/was fairly well-known, locally at least. Many of these classes meet two times a week for 75 minutes. Any class longer than the usual 50-minutes provides the librarian time to give classroom instruction as well as to provide some active learning exercises. Specifically, that means hands-on experience using specific biographical sources. These classes generally have between 15 and 20 students.

None of the hands-on activities direct the student to use the Internet. See the preceding chapter for suggestions as to how that can be incorporated.

Objectives of the Instruction:

- Reduce the library anxiety level which the average student harbors.

- Introduce students to the basics of Fact Tools and Finding Tools.

- Students will learn tips for locating categories of Fact and Finding Tools in the on-line catalog.

- Students will experiment with Boolean searching to achieve library efficiency.

- Students will engage in a hands-on library search activity.

- Students will share what they learned with classmates in the classroom setting.

Components of the Library Instruction:

Part 1 The classroom portion is at the beginning of the class period and lasts about 45 minutes. It includes a selection or all of the points which follow:

- Lead a get-acquainted activity so each student will meet one classmate. This type of activity leads to better learning and helps reduce any anxieties about being in the library classroom.

- Discuss the steps necessary to focus a topic; use some class participation here to stimulate involvement.

- Discuss the search strategy steps which any researcher should follow when conducting a library research project.

- Explain the characteristics of Fact Tools and Finding Tools (see *Learning the Library* for details). Be sure to stress that they are the same whatever the discipline.

- Since this class will be using biographical sources it is essential to discuss them generally. The information in the note below will help structure that portion of the classroom instruction.

> **NOTE:** A biography, to many people, is a book about a famous person and covers the life from birth. Others may think of a television documentary. Since most people don't have time to delve into book-length biographies when they want to place the person in a context and know about his place in time, culture, and society, the best place to turn is reference tools.
>
> Biographical dictionaries give brief data ranging from a sentence or two to several pages including a photograph. These dictionaries are the best starting point and are among the most used reference tools.
>
> There are three main types of biographical dictionaries and each may be further subdivided by time period, i.e., contemporary retrospective:
> > international or general;
> > national or regional; and
> > professional or occupational specialty.

- Topical keywords and what they will do to help a search.

- Boolean searching.

- Demonstration of efficient searching in the on-line catalog.

Part 2 The remaining 30 minutes of the class is a time for students to have practice using some of the biographical reference sources which they will need to use to complete the upcoming assignment.

At this point, the class moves to the reference area and each student is given a unique activity to be completed before the end of the period that day.

The assignment is in the form of an activity which is written out in detail and includes spaces for most of the responses/answers. It is also required that a journal be kept to record any search steps which cannot be included on the activity sheets. All of the results are to be turned in to the course instructor.

As a follow-through, the instructors have the students share information about the reference sources with classmates at the next class session. The reinforcement this provides has been well received by the instructors because their comments have been positive and encouraging.

Hands-on Activities for Students

A selection of 17 activities was created which requires the use of specific biographical sources. Each student works independently. All library-specific references have been removed so these activities can be photocopied and given to other classes in other libraries.

If certain other reference sources are wanted, those who have purchased the disk containing the activities can modify or revise to meet specific needs. They can also incorporate an Internet option into the activities.

Evaluation

The students do some of their own evaluating when they discuss their tool and the experiences of searching. The teaching faculty are encouraged to pass any comments about the library instruction session back to the librarians who conducted the class. The comments from both students and faculty have been encouraging and the time it takes to customize the work is worth the effort.

Variation for Other Classes

Many classes meet once a week for 2.75 hours and the following suggestions could be used to incorporate the additional time. More time can be spent on each of the points listed earlier as well as to introduce evaluation into the classroom portion. The few elements listed below will help structure the librarian's discussion of evaluation:

1. Discuss elements on the title page such as:
   - scope and content
   - author/compiler name with listing of degrees, position, earlier works, etc.
   - publisher
   - date including copyright and preface

2. Discuss elements to look for in the preface and introduction such as:

   - scope and content
   - rationale or methodology for selection
   - limitations of the work
   - intended audience

Researching Biographies

This activity is to search all the volumes of *Biography and Genealogy Master Index* (*BGMI*) in paper for the name Jerry Goldsmith. He is a well-known musician who writes music for Broadway and television productions, as well as films.

BGMI is a comprehensive index to current and retrospective biographical dictionaries and who's who publications. It is designed to be the best place to start a biographical search on people from every field of activity and from all areas of the world, especially when a person is not famous. The set references over 3 million people who have been listed in hundreds of reference sources.

> Want to save time? Promise yourself to keep a record of your search strategy. By doing this, you will not have to retrace your steps because you will always know what you have already done. Efficiency in your library work can be achieved when you **keep a log book** and write down every step you take, every subject and keyword you search, every reference source you search.

Step 1   Search the library catalog for the call number and location of *BGMI*.

Find the print volumes. Notice that annual supplements have been published since the mid-1980s.

Step 2   Search all the volumes for the name **Jerry Goldsmith**.

Step 3   Copy the abbreviations of the biographical titles and years in which you will find information on Goldsmith. How many entries are listed for him over the years?

Step 4   Refer to the inside covers of the *BGMI* to convert the abbreviations to full titles.

Step 5   Select the names of two biographical dictionaries in which you will find information about Goldsmith. One should be geared to his professional specialty.

Step 6   Search the catalog for call numbers and locations of these two biographical reference sources.

Step 7   Does the library have the editions(s) referred to in *BGMI*?

Step 8   Locate the two titles you selected and read the information about Jerry Goldsmith.

Step 9   Make a brief outline of the elements you could write about from your research in these two sources.

NOTE: Don't limit yourself to two sources when you are actually writing the obituary for your class assignment. This library activity requires only two so you learn the process.

Researching Biographies

This activity is to search the CD-ROM version of *Biography and Genealogy Master Index (BGMI)* for Charles Ringling, one of the brothers who started the Ringling Brothers' Circus.

BGMI is a comprehensive index to current and retrospective biographical dictionaries and who's who publications. It is designed to be the best place to begin your search for information on people from every field of activity from the beginning of time through today's news makers.

> Want to save time? Promise yourself to keep a record of your search strategy. By doing this, you will not have to retrace your steps because you will always know what you have already done. Efficiency in your library work can be achieved when you **keep a log book** and write down every step you take, every subject and keyword you search, every reference source you search.

Step 1   Ask a member of the library staff where you can search *BGMI* on CD-ROM.

Step 2   Access the database and then follow the instructions on the screen in order to proceed through the search steps to identify biographical sources for **Charles Ringling**.

Step 3   Use the name search rather than the extended search.

Type in the last name first. If you type in Charles before Ringling, you will be entered into the C section of the alphabet.

You may see more than one entry for a person, for example, without dates and with varying birth dates, initials, etc. It depends on the information in the biographical dictionaries.

Step 4   Notice in the alphabetical listing that there are also entries for

Ringling Brothers and **Ringling Family**.

Highlight the entry for **Ringling, Charles**.

How many different biographical reference works are listed for him?

Step 5   Go back to the alphabetical listing and select **Ringling Brothers**.

Are any of the references different? Keep in mind that you may find these useful when you are ready to write about Charles Ringling.

Step 6   Select one source which is general or national and select *Biography Index* as a second reference source. Print the references.

Step 7   Search the library catalog for call numbers and locations of these titles.

Step 8   If the library doesn't have the edition(s) or year(s) which were referred to in *BGMI*, look at your printout and select another title.

Step 9   Locate the titles you selected and read about Ringling.

NOTE: Don't limit yourself to two sources when you are actually writing the obituary for your class assignment. This library activity requires only two while you learn the process.

Researching Biographies

This activity is to search *Contemporary Authors* and locate biographical information on Lee Gutkind He is a well-known writer who has written on such diverse subjects as motorcycling and Thomas Starzl, a pioneer in organ transplant surgery. Gutkind is a faculty member in the English Department at the University of Pittsburgh.

***Contemporary Authors** is the most comprehensive of the biographical sources for twentieth-century writers; it covers more than 100,000 individuals. This series is published in print as well as on CD-ROM. If you need to cite the CD product as a source for your paper, use the following citation:* **Contemporary Authors on CD, Gale Research Inc., 1994.**

> Want to save time? Promise yourself to keep a record of your search strategy. By doing this, you will not have to retrace your steps because you will always know what you have already done. Efficiency in your library work can be achieved when you **keep a log book** and write down every step you take, every subject and keyword you search, every reference source you search.

Step 1   Locate the workstation where you can access *Contemporary Authors on CD*. It is easy to use and available options are displayed at the bottom of each screen.

Step 2   At the main menu, you will be asked to decide on the type of search, for example, author, title, subject, etc.

Select author name.

Step 3   Type **Gutkind**, the last name of the author, and the system will move to the first name which matches your request.

Step 4   Follow instructions on the screen to begin reading the information about **Lee Gutkind's** life and literary works.

Step 5   Examine the whole entry on the CD and decide which portions you should "mark text to print/save" in order to fulfill your information needs.

Step 6   Next, search the library catalog by subject to look for books which have been written about **Lee Gutkind.**

Step 7   Select a title, print the screen or write down the call number.

Locate the book on the shelves.

Step 8   Does the book focus on aspects that will help fulfill your information needs?

Researching Biographies

This activity is to search encyclopedias for biographical information on the South African poet, Dennis Brutus. Mr Brutus was exiled to Robben Island off the coast of Cape Town, South Africa, for 20 years.

*The **Encyclopedia Americana** and **Encylcopaedia Britannica** are two authoritative and well-known multi-volume general encyclopedias which provide brief summary information in all fields of knowledge. It is essential to search for encyclopedia information by first consulting the index volume(s). The reason is that special aspects of broader topics are usually included in the volume with the broader topic.*

Want to save time? Promise yourself to keep a record of your search strategy. By doing this, you will not have to retrace your steps because you will always know what you have already done. Efficiency in your library work can be achieved when you **keep a log book** and write down every step you take, every subject and keyword you search, every reference source you search.

Step 1   Search the library catalog for the location and call numbers of the *Encyclopedia Americana* and the *Encyclopaedia Britannica*.

Step 2   Locate the sets on the book shelves.

Step 3   Search index volumes of both for biographical articles on **Dennis Brutus**.

Step 4   Go to the volumes indicated and read the articles.

Is a listing of his writings included?

Is the reader alerted to any additional sources of biographical information? Note those which you think would be useful for further consultation.

Step 5   Search the most current encyclopedia yearbook (annual update volumes) to see if you find a listing for **Mr. Brutus**.

Step 6   Search the library catalog for **Dennis Brutus** both as an author and as a subject.

Step 7   What titles did you discover?

As an author?

As a subject?

Perhaps the dust jacket (paper cover on a book) will give additional information about him.

Researching Biographies

This activity is to search _International Who's Who_ for biographical material on China's paramount post-Mao leader, Deng Xiaoping.

The **International Who's Who** is the best source for brief biographical information on the world's most famous and influential men and women from all walks of life.

Want to save time? Promise yourself to keep a record of your search strategy. By doing this, you will not have to retrace your steps because you will always know what you have already done. Efficiency in your library work can be achieved when you **keep a log book** and write down every step you take, every subject and keyword you search, every reference source you search.

Step 1   Search the library catalog for the call number and location of the _International Who's Who_.

Step 2   Locate the latest, or at least a recent, edition. Some libraries may keep the latest edition at the reference desk.

Step 3   Spend a few minutes to skim the preface and introduction to determine:

a.   how the names of individuals were selected

b.   what restrictions were imposed for inclusion

c.   qualifications of the editors or editorial board

d.   reliability of the publisher

e. frequency of update

f. special features.

Step 4 Search for the name, **Deng Xiaoping**. It could also be written as **Teng Hsiao-p'ing** because of different romanization schemes. It is a good idea to search under both spellings.

Step 5 What categories of information are included in the *International Who's Who*?

Step 6 Has **Deng Xiaoping** worked in China other than as a politician?

Step 7 Go to the library catalog and do a subject search for the Chinese leader.

What form of the name does the catalog use? It is probably a good idea to look under both forms of the name as mentioned above.

Step 8 How many entries did you identify with this search?

Are any of them biographies?

Step 9 Most libraries have Far East specialists on their library faculty. Locate one of them and discuss what other sources there might be for information on the Chinese political leader.

Researching Biographies

This activity is to search *Notable Hispanic American Women* for information about the actress Raquel Welch whose father was a Bolivian immigrant.

Notable Hispanic American Women is a reference book which gives biographical information on women who have a South or Central American heritage.

> Want to save time? Promise yourself to keep a record of your search strategy. By doing this, you will not have to retrace your steps because you will always know what you have already done. Efficiency in your library work can be achieved when you **keep a log book** and write down every step you take, every subject and keyword you search, every reference source you search.

Step 1   Search the library catalog for the call number and location of the reference book *Notable Hispanic American Women.*

Step 2   Locate the book on the book shelves.

Step 3   Locate and read the article on **Raquel Welch**. Note particularly references to additional sources and photographs.

When you get to the end of the article, you will notice that a full-length biography has been written about her.

Step 4   Search the library catalog by subject for this full-length biography.

Who wrote the book?

Step 5   Locate the biography on the shelf and examine it for the points about:

    a.   the author's qualifications

    b.   type of publisher

    c.   documents consulted.

Step 6   The author of this work will undoubtedly reference articles in periodicals, articles in newspapers, oral interviews, etc.

These will be good leads for further research. Check them out.

Researching Biographies

This activity is to locate information on a local person who became mayor of your city. People who have not become newsworthy beyond a local community will not be indexed in the major reference tools so information has to be sought locally.

*An **archives** collects the recorded memory of a person or organization. Here is one example. A university or college archives therefore collects the corporate memory of the institution since it was established. This "memory" includes: (a) office files of presidents or Chancellors, deans, departments, etc.; (b) official publications; (c) lecture notes of professors; (d) student papers; (e) photographs; (f) films taken at football games; (g) anything and everything that relates to and tells the story of the institution or person.*

Want to save time? Promise yourself to keep a record of your search strategy. By doing this, you will not have to retrace your steps because you will always know what you have already done. Efficiency in your library work can be achieved when you **keep a log book** and write down every step you take, every subject and keyword you search, every reference source you search.

Step 1   Ask a librarian to help you identify local archives and historical societies. The following is a beginning checklist:

- local history room in a public library
- historical society (city or country)
- newspaper office
- municipal archives
- college or university archives
- corporate archives
- church archives

Step 2 The librarian will probably suggest that you telephone each of the above type of archives and find out if you need to make an appointment to go and search for material on your local personality. Be sure to get the specific name and address of each.

Step 3 Ask the staff in the various archives about any special rules or regulations concerning the use of archival materials. For example, you may not be able to make photocopies of the documents.

Step 4 Ask the staff in the various archives what other sources they would suggest for additional information.
Pursue those suggestions.

Step 5 The local newspaper will keep files which the journalists use when they are writing. Some papers maintain an archives/library and allow researches to access these materials.

NOTE: Finding information on a local personality will take time.

Researching Biographies

This activity is to search the electronic version of *PAIS* and locate information about Mikhail Gorbachev, the former head of the Communist Party and leader of the Soviet Union.

PAIS (Public Affairs Information Service) is an index to policy oriented literature in periodical articles, international government publications, as well as selected books. Fields covered are: business, economic and social conditions; public policy and administration; and international relations.

Want to save time? Promise yourself to keep a record of your search strategy. By doing this, you will not have to retrace your steps because you will always know what you have already done. Efficiency in your library work can be achieved when you **keep a log book** and write down every step you take, every subject and keyword you search, every reference source you search.

Step 1   Ask a librarian where the CD-ROM version of *PAIS* is located.

Step 2   Look for a sheet of searching tips; many libraries have prepared handouts for each of the CD-ROM databases which are available in the library.

Step 3   Assume you don't know the exact spelling of **Gorbachev** so begin by searching for the first few letters; use "Gorb" plus the symbol which allows for truncation. Sort through enough of the entries until you find the correct spelling used in this database.

Step 4   Next search for the whole surname. Use **Gorbachev**.

Step 5 Next search for the whole surname as a subject heading. Refer to the sheet with searching tips or the on-screen instructions about subject searching. Notice the decreasing number of hits as the search strategy gets more specific.

Step 6 Add the word "biography" to your search strategy and the number of hits are reduced dramatically. Look at these.

In which languages were the articles written? *PAIS* includes references in many languages.

Step 7 Print the results, or make hand notes in you log book so you'll have full citations when you begin to locate these sources.

Many of these sources will not be available in your local library. These indexes are not library specific .

Step 8 Locate the title of one periodical reference which has a biographical article on **Mikhail Gorbachev**. Which is it?

Search the library catalog which includes the listing of periodical titles in order to determine if the article is immediately accessible.

Step 9 Search the library catalog for the title of one book which you selected from the *PAIS* search.

Researching Biographies

This activity is to search *Notable American Women, The Modern Period* for biographical information on Beatrix Jones Farrand, reputed to be the finest woman landscape architect of her time.

Notable American Women, The Modern Period is a reference work which includes biographies of nearly 500 women who died between 1951 and 1975. It is a companion to **Notable American Women, 1607-1950.**

Want to save time? Promise yourself to keep a record of your search strategy. By doing this, you will not have to retrace your steps because you will always know what you have already done. Efficiency in your library work can be achieved when you **keep a log book** and write down every step you take, every subject and keyword you search, every reference source you search.

Step 1   Search the library catalog for the call number and location of the volumes of *Notable American Women.*

Step 2   Read the preface and introduction to find out:

a.   qualifications of the authors

b.   further information about the inclusion of individuals

c.   type of data that has been included for each biographee

d.   inclusion of sources and further bibliographies

e.   inclusion of photographs.

Step 3   In which title was **Beatrix Jones Farrand** included?

Step 4   Select one of the references which is listed to have further information on the life and works of **Mrs. Farrand**.

Step 5   Search the library catalog for call number and location.

Step 6   Also search the library catalog by subject for any books about **Beatrix Jones Farrand**.

How many do you find?

Step 7   Locate these books on the shelves. Follow leads which are included in the biographical references in these books.

Researching Biographies

This activity is to search the index to *the New York Times* for information about Julia Child. She is well-known to the American public for teaching us the art of French cooking. She has had several television series and is the author of a number of cookbooks. Search from 1990 through the curent issues of the paper index.

The New York Times is a newspaper which gives extensive coverage of national and international news. It has its own index called New York Times Index and it covers the entire life of the newspaper, since 1851. The index is arranged under subjects.

Want to save time? Promise yourself to keep a record of your search strategy. By doing this, you will not have to retrace your steps because you will always know what you have already done. Efficiency in your library work can be achieved when you **keep a log book** and write down every step you take, every subject and keyword you search, every reference source you search.

Step 1   Locate the *New York Times Index* in the reference area. If you have any difficulties, please speak with a staff member at the desk.

Step 2   Select the volume for 1990 and look under **Julia Child**; you will need to search under the surname.

Step 3   You will discover that persons are frequently indexed under the subject. In this case, you will be instructed to **SEE ALSO** headings like cooking, theater, etc.

This means you must turn to that part of the alphabetical sequence and search for a reference to **Julia Child** by the date indicated on the page where you were told to see another heading. All headings under a subject are arranged by date.

Step 4   Copy the information about date, section, and page of the *New York Times*. This will be essential in order to locate the article.

Step 5   Search the remaining years, 1991 to the present.

Step 6   Now you will need to locate the area of the library where the microfilm copies of the newspapers are kept. Libraries retain the back years of newspapers on film, not on paper.

Step 7   Locate the shelves or drawers which hold the years you need; take the rolls of film to a microfilm reader or reader-printer.

Thread the film on one of the microfilm readers. If this is your first experience, ask a staff member for assistance.

Step 8   Find the date, section, and page for each reference you want to read.

Step 9   Take notes about the biographical information your need on **Julia Child** or make a paper copy from the film. Again, a staff member will be available to assist you.

Researching Biographies

This activity is to search the *New York Times* full-text on CD-ROM for the past three years for biographical information on John C. Bogle, investment adviser and head of the Vanguard Group of Mutual Funds.

The New York Times is a newspaper which gives extensive coverage of national and international news. The paper index covers the entire life of the newspaper, since 1851. The past few years of the newspaper are now available full-text on CD-ROM.

Want to save time? Promise yourself to keep a record of your search strategy. By doing this, you will not have to retrace your steps because you will always know what you have already done. Efficiency in your library work can be achieved when you **keep a log book** and write down every step you take, every subject and keyword you search, every reference source you search.

Step 1   Ask a library staff member where you can search the full-text CD-ROM version of the *New York Times.*

Step 2   Read the instructions on the screens so you will know how to search. Ask if the library has prepared a help-sheet for users.

Step 3   Search for and locate anything about **John C. Bogle**.

Step 4   Read through the titles and move on to look at the full-text of some of these articles.

How many were included in the past three years?

Step 5   Print the articles which will be valuable as you write about this well-known personality in the mutual fund business.

Step 6   **Mr. Bogle** recently wrote a book on mutual fund investing.

Search the library catalog for this title.

Step 7   Search the library catalog by subject to see if anyone has written a book about Bogle.

Books by a person will be located by conducting an author search.

Books about a person will be located by conducting a subject search.

Researching Biographies

This activity is to search the *Biography Index* and identify biographical information on the mail order catalog executive, Lilian Vernon Katz.

Biography Index is a comprehensive guide to biographical material in books and periodical articles. This index does not contain the biographical material itself but identifies the location of biographies, autobiographies, letters, diaries, and pictorial works.

> Want to save time? Promise yourself to keep a record of your search strategy. By doing this, you will not have to retrace your steps because you will always know what you have already done. Efficiency in your library work can be achieved when you **keep a log book** and write down every step you take, every subject and keyword you search, every reference source you search.

Step 1   Search the library catalog to find the call number and location of the *Biography Index.*

Step 2   Search in the volumes from the middle 1980s to the present time for **Lilian Vernon Katz.** You will discover that you are referred to the entry under **Lilian Vernon** rather than under Katz.

Step 3   How many entries to do find for her in the last decade?

Step 4   Select two articles which have appeared in different periodicals.

Select one of the articles from the early 1980s.

For the second article, select the latest one to appear in the 1990s.

Step 5   Copy the full references so you can complete the search for information on the life and accomplishments of this enterprising business woman.

Step 6   Search the library catalog which includes periodical titles .

Determine if the library subscribes to those periodicals which you selected.

Step 7   Locate the volumes on the shelves.

Step 8   Find the articles and compare coverage based on the purposes of the periodical titles you selected.

Researching Biographies

**This activity is to search *American Men and Women of Science*
and *Current Biography* to locate biographical information on
Bernadine Healy, first female director of the National Institutes of
Health in 1991.**

*American Men and Women of Science; A Biographical Directory
of Today's Leaders in Physical, Biological, and Related Sciences*
*is a who's who type of biographical directory. About 130,000 names
are included in the latest edition.*

*Current Biography is a monthly publication which contains fairly
lengthy articles on noteworthy or newsworthy people of all nations,
professions, and occupations. Each article summarizes the lives and
accomplishments of the people,and includes a portrait as well as a
brief listing of sources for further information.*

Want to save time? Promise yourself to keep a record of your search strategy. By
doing this, you will not have to retrace your steps because you will always know what
you have already done. Efficiency in your library work can be achieved when you **keep
a log book** and write down every step you take, every subject and keyword you
search, every reference source you search.

Step 1   Search the library catalog for the call number and location of the volumes of
American Men and Women of Science.

Step 2   Find the two latest editions on the book shelves and select the volume which
will include the names beginning with the letter H.

Step 3   Locate Bernadine Healy.

          What types of information does this reference source provide? It seems you
          would not be able to write much of an obituary from the who's who type
          source.

Step 4   Using the steps followed to find the previous title, find the second reference
          source called *Current Biography*.

Step 5   Locate the biography of **Bernadine Healy**.

          Notice that there is a separate volume for each year since *Current Biography*
          began in 1940; each volume has its own index and there are also cumulated
          indexes for the earlier years.

Step 6   What types of information does this source provide?

Step 7   Compare the coverage of the two reference sources for your purpose of writing
          an obituary on **Bernadine Healy**.

Researching Biographies

This activity is to search *F&S Index plus Text* on CD-ROM for information on Anthony O'Reilly who is the CEO of the Heinz Corporation.

F&S Index plus Text is a CD-ROM product that contains information on all manufacturing and service industries and covers a wide range of business and technology related topics from over 1,000 trade and business journals, the business press, and government publications. It covers both international and United States business topics.

> Want to save time? Promise yourself to keep a record of your search strategy. By doing this, you will not have to retrace your steps because you will always know what you have already done. Efficiency in your library work can be achieved when you **keep a log book** and write down every step you take, every subject and keyword you search, every reference source you search.

Step 1   Ask a member of the reference staff where you can search the *F&S Index plus Text* on CD-ROM.

Step 2   Follow the instructions on the screen in order to proceed through the search steps. Also ask if the library has prepared a help sheet for users.

Notice what dates are included in this database.

Step 3   Take sufficient time to read and understand the screens which discuss the database and the retrieval system.

Step 4   It is possible that you'll need to search both **O'Reilly** and then **Oreilly** just to be sure you don't miss any entries.

Be sure to combine the personal name with Heinz because O'Reilly is fairly common.

Step 5   Follow instructions and look at the full text.

Notice that every occurrence of the search terms will be highlighted.

Step 6   Now, you choose the name of some other person to search in this database.

Write down the name of the person.

Record your search strategy and the results below.

Step 7   Search the World Wide Web for more company information. Larger companies will have their own site. Entering the company name in the Web search program will show whether there is a site. Financial data on many can be found in "Edgar," a database maintained by the US Securities and Exchange Commission, at http://www.sec.gov/edgarhp.htm

Researching Biographies

This activity is to search *CD NEWSBANK* for information about former pro-football coach Joe Bugel. Look especially for his connections to the city of Pittsburgh.

CD NEWSBANK provides complete text of current news and articles in regional US and Canadian newspapers and wire services from around the globe. Issues and events which make headlines in the United States and the world include:

- the environment
- health issues
- education
- international affairs
- social issues
- urban affairs
- science and technology
- the arts
- biography
- crime and the legal system
- sports
- world & national politics

Want to save time? Promise yourself to keep a record of your search strategy. By doing this, you will not have to retrace your steps because you will always know what you have already done. Efficiency in your library work can be achieved when you **keep a log book** and write down every step you take, every subject and keyword you search, every reference source you search.

Step 1   Ask at reference where you can access *CD NEWSBANK.*

Step 2   Follow the on-screen instructions in order to proceed through the search steps. The library may also have prepared a help sheet for users.

Take sufficient time to read and understand the screen which discuss the database and the retrieval system before you begin.

Step 3   Type in **Bugel's** name.

If you retrieve a large number of references you will want to revise the search and add Pittsburgh as well.

Step 4   Follow instructions to look at the full text.

Notice that every occurrence of the search terms will be highlighted.

Step 5   Now, you choose the name of some other sports personality to search in this database.

Write down the name of the person.

Record your search strategy and the results below.

Step 6   In what other type of reference source would you expect to locate biographical information on a sports personality?

Step 7   Locate at least one reference source in the library catalog.

Explain how you structured that search.

Name the source.

Researching Biographies

This activity is to search *Information Science Abstracts* and locate information on Tony Carbo Bearman, Dean of the School of Library and Information Sciences at the University of Pittsburgh and appointed by President Clinton to the National Information Infrastructure Advisory Council.

Information Science Abstracts *contains references and abstracts to the world's literature in librarianship, information science, and related fields. The database indexes journal articles, books, research reports, conference proceedings, and patents. It is produced in both online and printed versions.*

> Want to save time? Promise yourself to keep a record of your search strategy. By doing this, you will not have to retrace your steps because you will always know what you have already done. Efficiency in your library work can be achieved when you **keep a log book** and write down every step you take, every subject and keyword you search, every reference source you search.

Step 1   Ask at the reference desk where you can search the on-line version of *Information Science Abstracts.*

Step 2   Follow the instructions on the screen in order to proceed through the search process. Also ask if the library has prepared a help sheet for users.

Take sufficient time to read and understand the screens which discuss the database and the retrieval system.

Step 3   Type in **Bearman.**

There is a David Bearman who is also in the information field so you will undoubtedly find references to him. Be sure to distinguish between the two.

Step 4   Read through all of the abstracts in order to get a feeling for her philosophy of information.

Is there mention of the national offices or appointments to high-level commissions?

Step 5   Print the abstracts and citations for those which would be useful background for writing something biographical.

Step 6   While you are searching this database, look for some other name.

Write down the name of the person you select.

Record your search strategy, and the results.

Step 7   Speculate what other types of sources you would look into for additional information on Toni Carbo Bearman.

What are they?

Step 8   Search the library catalog to determine if there are any books written by or about her that would help you in your quest for biographical information.

Record the results.

Researching Biographies

This activity is to search *Current Biography* and locate information on Mario LeMieux, the well known hockey star who plays with the Penguins.

Current Biography is a monthly publication which contains fairly lengthy articles on noteworthy or newsworthy people of all nations, professions, and occupations. Each article summarizes the lives and accomplishments of the people, includes a portrait as well as a brief listing of sources for further information.

Want to save time? Promise yourself to keep a record of your search strategy. By doing this, you will not have to retrace your steps because you will always know what you have already done. Efficiency in your library work can be achieved when you **keep a log book** and write down every step you take, every subject and keyword you search, every reference source you search.

Step 1   Search the library catalog for the call number and location of *Current Biography*.

Step 2   Consult the indexes and locate the volume which includes a biography of the Penguin star, **Mario LeMieux.**

Step 3   Quickly skim the article and make an outline of the aspects of Mario LeMieux's life which are covered.

Does any aspect seem to have been overlooked?

Step 4   What additional sources are listed at the end of the biography?

Step 5   Locate one of these sources.

Document the steps you follow to locate this additional biographical information.

Step 6   Compare the information found in *Current Biography* and the source you selected in the previous step.

Step 7   Speculate about other sources that would need to be consulted in order to write an obituary.

List them.

Speak with a reference librarian if you need some more ideas.

Business Information on the Internet

MARCIA KING-BLANDFORD

Instruction Coordinator
CARLSON LIBRARY, THE UNIVERSITY OF TOLEDO

Circumstances for the Instruction Session:

The Instruction Coordinator approached the English Department about using the following library instruction presentation for the course ORGANIZATIONAL REPORT WRITING. This is a course for undergraduate business majors and meets their English composition requirement. The presentation was developed in conjunction with the English Department and was taught as part of a pilot program during the summer of 1996; at least 10 sections continue to be taught each quarter. The presentation was developed to create a real-life approach to searching the Internet to retrieve business information. The retrieved information could be used to develop in-house and business memos, reports, press releases, and competitive assessments.

For the hands-on portion of this instruction session, the students can either be put into "task forces" to work as a group or they can work independently. The pre-searched topics for the Internet searching assignments are included in this chapter. The students are required to document any print and electronic sources used in accord with the appropriate writing style, such as APA, MLA, etc.

The instruction session is held in one of the University's computer classrooms which allows 24 students working on individual workstations. The session is held during one of the normal class times—the ORGANIZATIONAL REPORT WRITING class meets for 75 minutes twice a week. This instruction session is geared for a 75 minute time slot. If the students are Internet literate, the instruction session can either be shortened to 50-minutes and focusing specifically on retrieving business resources or adding more searching time.

To help decide about the level of Internet searching skills of both the class and the course instructor, some questions are asked when the instructional session is scheduled and during the opening minutes of this Internet training. Examples of questions are: Are you currently using email? Do you have a computer at home or where you work? Are you familiar with assessing the Internet? If yes, how much time during the week are you searching the Internet?

It is required that the course instructor be present. The ongoing working relationship with the English Department has supported and reinforced this requirement. The instruction librarians take the initiative to keep in continuous telephone and/or email contact with the teaching faculty in the English Department.

Objectives of the Instruction:

- Introduce students to searching the Internet to retrieve business information.
- Identify the types and categories of information that must be evaluated and illustrate various online evaluation guidelines.
- Introduce help screens, FAQs, and other resources that can be utilized to assist users on the Internet.
- Provide a hands-on opportunity to search and retrieve Internet business information.

Components of the Instruction:

TEACHING RESOURCES FOR COURSE INSTRUCTORS:
A Checklist for Preparing an Internet Instruction Session, *Computers in Libraries,*
> v. 16, no. 3, March 1996, p. 24

Understanding WWW Search Tools by Jian Liu, Reference Department, IUB Libraries
> http://www.indiana.edu/~librcsd/search/

PART I. HOW DO I BEGIN? (8 minutes)
Use the University's homepage to show the standard features of a homepage If your library, school, college, etc., does not have a homepage, you can start with the homepage of any site you like. You may want to begin with one of the government sites, like the White House, or your state government's homepage, or one of the identified business resources. Any site works fine.

INTRODUCE THE LANGUAGE OF THE INTERNET.
Illustrate pull down menus, icons, buttons, hot links, page, scrolling, arrows, etc. Because this terminology can be confusing to new users, it is a good idea to make a handout of terminology and/or inform them of the glossaries in the following:
> 1. A Web site glossary of Internet terms from Ithaca College Library
>   http://www.ithaca.edu/library/Training/intro.html
> 2. Bolner and Poirier, *The Research Process : books and beyond.* Dubuque, Iowa, Kendall/Hunt Publishing, c1997.

PART II. SEARCHING THE INTERNET   (15 minutes)
Keep the instruction simple and be brief; give only the very basics so students have enough information to get started.

> Special Note: Electronic information retrieval is *subject* searching vs. *keyword* searching.

A.   SUBJECT OR TOPIC SEARCHING APPROACH:
> Begin a subject or topic search by using the NET SEARCH button.

> **Illustrate** one of the net directories :

Give the definition of a net directory and show how it is used.
Show an example of Yahoo, http://www.yahoo.com
Select the BUSINESS category to show the classified hierarchical subject searching approach

Illustrate one of the search engines :
Give the definition of a search engine and show how it is used.
Show an example such as AltaVista, http://altavista.digital.com/
or, Infoseek, http://www.infoseek.com
Select a topic or keyword to illustrate the keyword approach

Suggested reference: Understanding WWW Search Tools by Jian Liu, Reference Dept., IUB Libraries
http://www.indiana.edu/~librcsd/search/

B.   SEARCH USING A SPECIFIC ADDRESS:
Begin a search using a specific URL showing either the OPEN button, or the pull down menu under FILE, or typing over the LOCATION.

URL (Uniform Resource Locator)
This is unique to the site; it represents an IP address that is really 32 bit in 4 sections. An IP address looks like this 152.160.1.36 *Detroit News*; a URL is easier to remember than a string of numbers.

The standard format of a URL:
protocol ://www.host computer.domain

The protocol can be either http://www or telnet or gopher.
The protocol is a series of computer programs and routines which two or more computers share when they are linked.

The host computer is specific to the site. The host is the geographic and name of the organization that owns and maintains the particular computer system.

The domain can be either .edu, .com, .gov, .org, to name the most common. It helps define what type of group sponsors the site, e.g.,
    commercial (.com),
    government (.gov),
    education (.edu), or an
    organization (.org).

"**Create**" and search a specific URL.
Suggestions: The White House, http://www.whitehouse.gov
                NBC/Microsoft, http://www.msnbc.com
                USA Today newspaper, http://www.usatoday.com

Emphasize that URLs can be case sensitive. If a URL has both upper and lower case letters, it must be typed as it was created.

Demonstrate BOOKMARKS. Once users know how to create the standard format for the URL, they can search for specific sites without using a search engine.

Create BOOKMARKS. They can easily be created by using the pull down menu under this heading. A Bookmark keeps the site readily available. That way the user can access the site without having to retype the URL.

PART III. WHAT YOU WILL FIND—EVALUATE INFORMATION AND SOURCES (8 minutes)

Special Note: *Anyone* can put information out on the Internet; therefore, each user must examine the validity of the information retrieved.

Access a site that provides evaluation guidelines. Suggest these:
T is for Thinking, Ithaca College Library, J. Henderson,
Webmaster http://www.ithaca.edu/library/Training/hott.html

Thinking Critically about World Wide Web Resources by Esther Grassian,
UCLA Library
http://www.library.ucla.edu/libraries/college/instruct/critical.htm

Identify the criteria used to evaluate information while the class is viewing the site.

Suggested handout. Write some of the URL addresses for evaluative tools on the board and/or have printed to distribute. Suggest that students add one as a Bookmark.

PART IV. BUSINESS INFORMATION SOURCES (35 minutes)

SUGGESTED BACKGROUND RESOURCES FOR INSTRUCTORS:
Tennant, Roy. *Crossing the Internet threshold : an instructional handbook.* 2nd ed.
Berkeley, CA : Library Solutions Press, c1994.
Peete, Gary R. *Business resources on the Internet : a hands-on workshop. 2nd printing, minor revisions.* Berkeley, CA : Library Solutions Press, c1995.

Illustrate both the print and corresponding electronic resources to the class. Provide one print source for two to three students to share. When the Internet site is retrieved, circulate each corresponding print resource to a cluster of students to examine while the Internet resource is examined. Students can be asked some questions about the print resources as the class examines the Web resource.

Assure the class that this demonstration is not meant to be comprehensive or evaluative. These sites were chosen as examples to illustrate the breadth and limitations of Web resources. As the class examines these sites, the students will be using the evaluative guidelines to assess the validity of the information retrieved.

LOCATING BUSINESSES:

Print Source: *AT & T 800 Toll-Free Directory*

Internet Source: ATT & T Toll-Free Internet Directory, http://www.tollfree.att.net
This site provides access to more than 150,000 businesses and organizations; each with its own toll-free number.

Internet Source: Yellow Pages, http://s7.bigyellow.com
America's national Yellow Pages : access to over 16.5 million businesses in the United States.

Begin with a look at the homepage for one of the sites.
Point out the advertising and some of the hot links of interest, such as date of latest revision, what the site includes, FAQs, and search tips.

FAQs (Frequently Asked Questions) and Help.

Some sites will have a FAQ. This is usually a place to check if users are having any problems searching the site and/or retrieving information from the site. The usual format for a FAQ is a series of questions and answers. This is a good way to gain information about how the site is organized.

Additional help may also be available. Reliable sites will give you tips on searching and/or a telephone number/email to help answer your search questions.

Illustrate a search by corporate name. Take a suggestion from the class, or suggest using Wendy's.

FINDING COMPANY INFORMATION:

Print Source: *Hoover's handbook of American companies.*
Austin, Tex. : Reference Press, c1995.

Internet Source: http://www.hoovers.com

Illustrate how the print source defines its scope and coverage in the preface of the print volume.

Ask questions about the types of information found using the evaluation guidelines. Suggest questions like, Where can you find what companies are included on the Web site? Which resource, print or electronic, includes more companies?

Search by a company name, such as **General Motors**. Illustrate how the information retrieved is very brief. If one requires more detailed information you must "subscribe" and pay for the information.

Internet Source   Industry Research Desk Website, http://www.virtualpet.com/industry/
This site will provide access to information about business, industry, factories, manufacturing, SIC codes, NAICS, government information, and industry profiles.

Illustrate how the site is organized and provides access to other sites they might have already used. The site serves as a "one stop shop" for searching for business information.

FINDING GOVERNMENT INFORMATION:

Print Source: U.S. Census from Bureau of the Census
Internet Source: http://www.census.gov/

Internet Source: http://www.marvel.gov
                    telnet   marvel.loc.gov

Illustrate the use of statistical information. Since census information is free and one of the most commonly used sources for statistical information, this is a user-friendly format. Suggest *Women owned businesses*, as a search example. The results are not only reports and statistics but access to the monthly newsletter, *Census and you*.

Illustrate the TELNET format of information versus what students find in World Wide Web (WWW) format. Telnet requires the searcher to use the software of the particular computer that was linked. The appearance is not consistent and the mouse probably can not be used. This is a good illustration of what Internet access looked like to its users before the Web browsers were available.

FINDING NEWSPAPERS:

Print Source: *New York Times*
Internet Source: http://nytimes.com

Print Source: *USA Today*
Internet Source: http://www.usatoday.com

Illustrate how only part of the newspaper is accessible through the web. **Illustrate** how you can "subscribe." Information may not always be free.

FINDING STATISTICAL INFORMATION:

Print Source: *Statistical Abstract of the United States*
Internet Source: http://www.census.gov/stat_abstract/

This is a core reference tool with a wealth of information and its easy-to-use format; it is available in either print or electronic form. The statistics (over 1400 tables and graphs) cover a wide variety of popular topics in the areas of business, social, economic, and international fields.

Illustrate how the information is indexed by tables in the print format. **Select** a search by category and then page through showing the actual text of the electronic resource compared with the text of the print resource.

OTHER SITES TO TRY:

www.ohiolink.edu for access to Ohio newspapers
www.oplin.org for Ohio public libraries
www.ohio.gov for Ohio government

Hands-on Searching (10-15 minutes)

While the students are searching their topics or just practicing, remind them about Help menus and FAQs:

A.   Help menus.

Help is available electronically via Help screens. As the class is searching, illustrate the different approaches to HELP menus.

B.   FAQs

Some sites will have a FAQ. This is usually a place to check if you are having any problems searching the site and/or retrieving information from the site. The usual format for an FAQ is a series of questions and answers. This is a good way to gain information about how the site is organized.

It is useful to distribute "The Glossary of Terms..." referred to in **Part I.** If your library has a Web site, print copies of this as it makes another good handout since the URL will be available for students to remember. The information listed in **Part IV. Business Resources** is distributed to the class as a handout. "Information Retrieval as a Work Flow Process" is a useful outline to distribute as a starting point for the Task Force assignments. It is simply one example of how a student can approach the electronic research process; the handout is included in this chapter. It is advisable to distribute handouts at the end of the session so the students won't be distracted from the presentation.

SAMPLE RESEARCH ASSIGNMENTS FOR TASK FORCES

For each of the following Internet research assignments, no cost figures need to be included. Sites are suggested for each assignments. The students must cite electronic sources using the appropriate APA or MLA style.

Web site for electronic citing:
Purdue University, Writing Lab
http://owl.english.purdue.edu
Recommended print resource:
Li, Xia and Nancy B. Crane. *Electronic style : a guide to citing electronic information.* Westport : Meckler, c1993.

Evaluation

Distribute an evaluation form to each student and to the course instructor to be completed at the end of the instructional session. The form is included at the end of this chapter.

Telephone the course instructor after the instructional session to get any additional feedback and to encourage repeating the session during the next quarter.

STUDENT(S)..

Task Force A Internet Research Assignment

Read the following statements carefully before you begin searching. No cost figures need to be included.

Your company is debating whether mammograms and prostrate screening should be part of the company's health package. You are asked to participate in a task force to make a recommendation. At this point, top management wants only the pros and cons. They have asked you to pay particular attention to offering this benefit to those in the workforce who are 40 and over.

Suggested sites to investigate:

http://www.cancer.org
http://www.graylab.ac.uk
http://www.prostrate-online.com

Task Force B Internet Research Assignment

Read the following statements carefully before you begin searching. No cost figures need to be included.

> You have been asked to sit on the task force that will make a recommendation for or against an on-site day care facility. This your company has a predominately female workforce, top management wants to know if this would be beneficial to recruiting and retaining female employees.

Suggested sites to investigate:

http://www.liveandlearn.com/daycare.pick.html
http://www.el.com/aoc/hinfo3.html

Task Force C Internet Research Assignment

Read the following statement carefully before you begin searching. No cost figures need to be included.

Your company has decided it is time to disband its affirmative action plan. You have been asked to look at the pros and cons of this action.

Suggested site to investigate:

http://www.berkshire-aap.com/articles.htm

STUDENT(S)..

Task Force D Internet Research Assignment

Read the following statements carefully before you begin searching. No cost figures need to be included.

- Your company has been hit with a sexual harassment policy. During the trial, it was revealed that your company does not have a sexual harassment policy in place. You have been assigned to work on making recommendation for defining what a corporate sexual harassment policy should contain.

Suggested sites to investigate:

http://www.Baclaw.com
http://www.aetc.af.mil/sh-policy.html

Task Force E Internet Research Assignment

Read the following statements carefully before you begin searching. No cost figures need to be included.

- In an effort to downsize, the corporate administration has decided to outsource all clerical employees. You have been asked to make recommendation on an appropriate plan to help the clerical employees make this transition.

Suggested site to investigate:

http://www.ndma.com

Information Retrieval As A Work Flow Process

What do I need to know?	Statistics, Laws, Competitive Information, Regulations, Budget, Staffing
	Time Frame: current, or historical, or, future
	Who is the audience?
⇓	
What do I have available?	Electronic access, human resources, public library reference desk, local academic libraries, commercial document delivery
⇓	
What is not available?	Sometimes no information will be available to use.
⇓	
How do you begin?	Specific site to use with a known URL, or, Browsing or searching by topic utilizing a Search Directory or Search Engine. ⇓
Information gathered?	Texts, graphs, contact names, articles, chapters, books, conference papers, statistics, laws/legislation, newspaper articles, company history, peers
⇓	
Information evaluation?	Is this information authentic, reliable, timely? Who is responsible for generating this information? Do I have any doubts about any of the information gathered? Recheck doubtful information using possible print resources.
⇓	
Information cited?	Give credit where credit is due. Always include dates.
⇓	
Information synthesis?	Critical examination and review of the information gathered.
⇓	
End product ⇒	Report, memos, email, letter, presentation, etc.

Evaluation Form

Please complete an evaluation of this instruction class.

Use this scale to rate your opinion about the Internet instruction:

    1—Not satisfied
    2—Somewhat satisfied
    3—Satisfied
    4—Very satisfied
    5—Excellent

_____ Presentation   ____ Computer Demonstration   ____ Pace

_____ Content   ____ Handouts   ____ Class length

Please complete the following sentences:

1. To improve this instructional session, I would…

2. I learned how to….

3. I still do not know how to …

4. The handouts were…

5. If a friend asked about this Internet instruction, what would you do?
   _____ recommend
   _____ not recommend

6. Please indicate whether or not you understand the following terms as they were used during the instructional session. Write **Yes** or **No** by each.

_____ Internet	_____ URL
_____ homepage	_____ Search engine
_____ World Wide Web	_____ Net search
_____ Bookmark	_____ hot link
_____ keyword searching	_____ FAQs

   Other comments:

Money and Banking—On the Internet

JANET MCNEIL HURLBERT

Associate Professor & Head, Instructional Services and Archives
LYCOMING COLLEGE, WILLIAMSPORT, PA

Circumstances for the Instruction Session:

An economics professor wished to incorporate more emphasis on electronic resources in a traditional upper division undergraduate money and banking course.

The class of 25 students will attend two 65-minute library sessions. After each library instruction session, the students must complete a worksheet which will be graded.

Goals:

- To enable all students in the class to become familiar with Internet capabilities and information: Web sites, discussion lists, search engines, and home pages.
- To review print and CD-ROM resources in business and economics to support research for a short paper.

Objectives of the Instruction:

- Develop successful searching skills and processes on the Internet using search engines.
- Become familiar with the instructional aspects of utilizing an informational home page.
- Evaluate sites on the Internet for relevant informational content.
- Compare and contrast information gained on the Internet to information found in traditional library resources and integrate these into a research project.

Components of the Library Instruction:

Part 1 PREPARATION:

1. A week before the first library session, students complete an Internet Readiness Survey (included in this chapter and may be photocopied) so that the librarian and the instructor can plan the session based on the familiarity of the class with the resources to be covered. Question number four, which asks students to describe other library resources they have used in the past, helps the librarian plan for the second library session which concentrates on traditional resources. Although students claim to be

quite competent in the library, they are seldom able to recall more than one or two specific resource titles.

The librarian uses this information to place the students in working groups for the class periods. The hope is that more and less experienced students will be working together in these small groups and that the more experienced will assist the less experienced.

When students enter the room, they will see their group assignments posted on the tables. Students will be asked to discuss with each other how competent they feel on the Internet. No exercise is to be considered complete until each student in a group feels that he or she can understand it. The students should rotate at the keyboard during the hands-on activities. The most experienced student is assigned the role of coach.

2. The classroom professor tells students to register for an email account before the first library session. An internal Internet newsgroup list is established for the class through the Computer Center and this discussion list will eventually be used by the instructor to enable students to continue discussions of topics mentioned in class. The librarian posts a welcoming message on the list before the first library session.

3. The instructor and librarian select five to six sites on the Internet especially relevant to money and banking and create a home page for the class that can be linked from the library home page as well as the instructor's home page.

4. Handouts are prepared for the class on the following:

    1. Critically analyzing information on the Web; or mounting the following Web sites on the library and class home pages
     (See handout "Evaluating Sites on the Web")
        T is for Thinking   http://www.ithaca.edu/library/Training/hott.html
        Evaluating Quality on the Net
        http://www.tiac.net/users/hope/findqual.html
        Thinking Critically about the World Wide Web
        http://www.library.ucla.edu/libraries/college/instruct/critical.htm
    2. Netiquette (included in this chapter)
    3. Library resources other than the Internet—print, CD-ROM, online.
    4. A recent article comparing search engines found in an Internet periodical. (An example is Tweney's "Searching Is My Business: A Gumshoe's Guide to the Web," in *PC World*, December 1996)

Part 2 PRESENTATION:

Session One:
The librarian presents a brief overview of the Internet according to the level of the class as indicated on the Internet surveys. This includes a discussion of critically evaluating

information on the Internet. Examples of good and bad sites are projected and the librarian leads the class in a collective evaluation of the information presented according to the handout on evaluating Web sites, entitled "Evaluating Sites on the Web; or, Whose Information Is It Anyway?"

A verbal netiquette quiz of two or three questions is given to bring attention to acceptable ways of communicating with each other on their class discussion list. (About 20 minutes)

Group Activity: Students in their assigned groups go to the computer stations and learn how to log on to their discussion list. They also examine the home page that has been established for the class. Each group tries out one of the sites on this home page and gives an overview of its content to the rest of the class. (About 15 minutes)

The librarian then brings the class back into a presentation mode and explains the concept of search engines and the difference between surfing and searching for relevant material on the 'Net by using a logical search process that is pertinent no matter what search engine is utilized. The librarian also illustrates by showing searching procedures on *one* search engine. (About 15 minutes)

Group Activity: The class returns to the computers in their assigned groups and tries out the same keyword in several search engines to see how different the results can be. Then each group is asked to find a site on a topic in money and banking by using a search engine. They are to evaluate it according to the handout "Evaluating Sites on the Web; or, Whose Information Is It Anyway?" and then share their observations with the class. (About 15 minutes)

The students are then given their assignment worksheets (included in this chapter) which are to be done individually as homework.

Session Two:
The second library class focuses on more traditional sources—print, online, CD-ROM. The session may begin with brief reminders about selecting and narrowing a topic as well as a demonstration of a new service to which the library subscribes or an especially useful print source in money and banking.

Students are then asked to try each information station that has been established based on the appropriate sources, and locate one or two references pertaining to their selected topics. This may include actually going to the stacks and retrieving a useful book or finding a journal article. [Sometimes free photocopying is provided during the class period to encourage students to make good use of their time]

The librarian reassembles the class for the last 15 minutes to share what materials have been found and to see if students have refined topics based on available resources.

Usually during this session, students have begun with general topics such as the Federal Reserve system, savings and loans, or the stock market. By the end of class, they have begun to focus on topics such as e-money, a particular court case, or junk bonds. Students are once again given an assignment which is to be completed individually as homework.

Evaluation:

Making sure each group is on task at the Internet terminals is challenging. It helps if there is another library staff member, a qualified student worker, or the professor with whom you are working who can assist.

The activity worksheets that are turned in by students are graded by the librarian, and the points earned count as a homework assignment for the course. Students are expected to use the Internet and their newsgroup list throughout the semester, so they must master the material.

Internet Readiness Survey

Please answer the following questions.

1. In your own words, explain what the Internet is.

2. Have you ever used the Internet?

_____yes _____no

If your answer is "yes" to question 2, answer these questions:

a. How frequently do you use the Internet?

_____used once

_____used a few times

_____use often

b. Have you ever conducted a search on the Internet using any search engine?

AltaVista	_____ yes	_____no
WebCrawler	_____ yes	_____no
InfoSeek	_____ yes	_____no
Other_____	_____ yes	_____no

c. What information sites on the Internet do you like to use? List them.

d. Have you been part of a newsgroup or discussion list?

_____yes _____no

e. List courses you have taken that utilized Internet resources.

f. Do you have an Internet connection to the World Wide Web in the residence hall or through a home modem. _____yes _____no

3. Have you used email? _____yes _____no

4. Consider library resources OTHER than the Internet. List and briefly describe the kinds of sources you have used.

NETIQUETTE—a quick overview

Your Responsibility——
- Check e-mail often.
- Keep messages in your mail box to a minimum.
    Never assume your e-mail cannot be read by others.

Electronic Communications——
- Keep messages to the point.
- Focus on one subject per message.
    Capitalize only when grammar demands. Capitalizing whole words that are not titles is generally termed as SHOUTING!
    Remember that e-mail is easily forwarded. Your message could be around the world in a few minutes.
    Be careful about using sarcasm and humor. Remember that people do not see your face or hear your voice.
- Don't forward personal mail without the sender's permission.
    Follow all rules for fair use and copyright.

Listserv and Mailing List Discussion Groups——
- Don't post messages until you see what the list is really like.
- Follow the rules and guidelines for the list.
- Remember that people on a list come from all over the world—cultures are different, references may be misunderstood.
- Don't "flame" by sending inflammatory or obscene messages. You could lose your access to the net.
- Keep your comments relevant. Respond to an *individual* if the comment is not applicable to the interests of the whole list.

Evaluating Sites on the Web; or,
Whose information is it anyway?

Developed by Lisette Ormsbee, Lycoming College Library

Information is a product of human interpretation of data and other interpretations as presented in various formats whether print, electronic, or other published material. The American Library Association publishes a pamphlet entitled *Evaluation Information: A Basic Checklis t*. Its treatment of *source evaluation* is relevant across formats, whether print, electronic, or multimedia. The checklist which follows is based on that of ALA.

• What **type** of source is it? Scholarly, popular, governmental, private, for-profit, non-profit?

• What are the **author's** or **producer's** qualifications for this topic—education, experience, occupation, position, affiliation, publications?

• **When** was the information published?

• In which **country** was it published?

• What is the **reputation** of the publisher, producer, or distributor? Are they known?

• Was the material **reviewed** or **edited** for publication?

• Does the source show political or cultural **bias**?

• Is there a bibliography or other forms of **documentation** included?

• What is the best format for accessing the information, considering cost, time, ease of use?

In addition, when you are dealing with Web sites, consider:

• Is this a personal or official home page?

• Can you get back to the parent home page (say a university, business, or sponsoring agency)? Even if you can't link to the parent home page, do you know what or who it is?

• What date is listed on the page for creation or revision? Can you tell how old the information is that appears on the page? What date did *you* visit the site?

• Have you cited the URL (the Uniform Resource Locator or address of the site)?

In the vague place where virtual reality and scholarly research intersect, we need to determine what we have found and be able to identify the elements of a home page in order to properly "cite the site." Not all web pages have been created with attention to those elements; a search may drop you off in the middle of an apparently unauthored, untitled work with no clear sense of authority. Such information should be suspect, despite its enticing content.

Economics 220—Money and Banking

Worksheet 1   Due.................

Step 1 Choose a topic (or combination of topics) within the discipline of money and banking.

Execute a search using two different search engines.
Compare and contrast the two search engines according to search capabilities and results.

Topic chosen: _____

_____

Search engines used: _____

Evaluation:

_____

_____

_____

_____

_____

_____

_____

Step 2 Examine the Web site entitled _____ that is linked on the class home page. Write a description of the contents of this site that can be mounted on the class home page.

_____

_____

_____

_____

_____

Step 3 Using the search engines, select one new Web site that can support the information needs of this Money and Banking course. Evaluate the site using the guidelines in "Evaluating Sites on the Web, or Whose Information Is It Anyway?" (This site will be posted under your name on the class home page.)

Web site name _____

Web site address (URL) _____

Web site evaluation:

_____

_____

_____

_____

_____

_____

_____

_____

_____

_____

Step 4 Recommend three topics that would be suitable for a short research paper for this class. The paper is only 4-5 pages in length so the topic should not be too broad, and you should be able to collect most of the information from this library and
the Internet.

Note: The bibliography will need to contain both journal articles and Web sites.

Check these sources listed below to get ideas and to test your ideas:
• *Business Index*
• Reference materials such as: [Library of Congress numbers are included]
  Survey of Social Science. Economics Series.— HB61.S94.1991
  Encyclopedia of Banking & Finance— HG151.E63.1992
  The New Palgrave Dictionary of Money & Finance— HG151.N48.1992
• Search engines on the Internet as well as the Web sites on the class home page

Write a justification statement for each topic which explains why it is an appropriate topic for this course and explains how materials may be found to research the topic. Please rank the topics.

Best choice:

_____

_____

_____

_____

_____

_____

Second choice:

_____

_____

_____

_____

_____

Third choice:

_____

_____

_____

_____

_____

_____

Step 5 Post a message to the class newsgroup that describes what you learned from completing this assignment, and what difficulties you had. Print and attach a copy of that posting to this worksheet.

YOU ARE NOW CERTIFIED TO DRIVE ON THE INTERNET HIGHWAY for ECON 220–Money and Banking.

Economics 220—Money and Banking

Worksheet 2   Due................

Step 1 Examine one of the web sites chosen by a classmate and posted on your class home page. Evaluate the Web site using "Evaluating Sites on the Web; or, Whose Information Is It Anyway?"

List the Web site chosen.
Write the Web site in correct bibliographic form. See the class home page.

Evaluation:

Step 2 Use Dow Jones Information Retrieval to locate two sources of data that would support what you are learning in class and/or that relate to the paper that you will be writing for the class. Give the type of data and write a detailed description.

Type of data:

Description:

Type of data:

_____

Description:

_____

_____

_____

_____

_____

_____

_____

Step 3 Post a message to your class newsgroup telling members of the class about what you have located on Dow Jones.

Staple the message to this worksheet.

Step 4 Start research for your paper.
State your research topic:

_____

_____

_____

Identify one article citation from *Business Index.* Copy the citation and staple it to this worksheet. Indicate whether or not this library has the journal and explain why you feel the article is a good source to use for your paper.

Does the library have the journal? _____

Why is this article a good source?

_____

_____

_____

Identify one article citation using *Social Sciences Index*: Copy the citation and staple it to this worksheet. Indicate whether or not this library has the journal and explain why you feel the article is a good source to use for your paper.

Does the library have the journal? _____

Why is this article a good source?

_____

_____

_____

Identify one article in *Carl Uncover*: Copy the citation and staple it to this worksheet. Indicate whether or not this library has the journal and explain why you feel the article is a good source to use for your paper.
Does the library have the journal? _____

Why is this article a good source?

_____

_____

_____

Step 5   Select and read a <u>good</u> journal article on the topic of your research paper. Photocopy the article and attach it to the worksheet.

Write a letter to me describing your topic; how you plan to approach the topic (how you plan to narrow it, what subtopics you will cover, etc.); and what research strategy you will use. Include the names of specific Web sites as well.

There is space for your letter on the next page.

Dear _____ :

_____

_____

_____

_____

_____

_____

_____

_____

_____

_____

_____

Sincerely,

Career Exploration and Development

IRENE WEINER

Reference and Bibliographic Instruction Librarian
SCHOOL OF PROFESSIONAL AND GRADUATE STUDIES
Baker University, Baldwin City, Kansas

Circumstances for the Instruction Session:

As part of its overall mission to enhance student opportunities, a local community college has incorporated a six week session on career exploration within its Psychology Department. The class meets once a week for three hours. One class session meets in the library and is designed to demonstrate all the research components of deciding on a career and finding a job. The instructors in the department are very anxious that students have access, not only to traditional library sources, but also to the web. The class size can range from 15 to 25 students; it can be divided into working groups for a hands-on activity.

Objectives of the Instruction:

To teach students how to find information that will help them:
- determine their career objectives
- finance their education
- locate the appropriate school for their major
- write a resume
- look for a job

Components of the Instruction:

PART 1 PREPARATION:

Prepare a lengthy handout for print resources that is presented in a question and answer format. This will establish the class outline, indicating how research will be beneficial in answering questions. See the handout included in this chapter.
For example:

Where can I find out about careers?
Which schools offer the programs I need?
How will I be able to finance my education?
Where can I get some experience before I graduate?
How do I write a resume?
Where do I look for a job?
What do I know about the companies that are hiring?
What happens if I have to relocate for a job?

In addition, prepare another handout which lists websites that can be used to answer the same questions. Organize them in the same way that the printed sources are organized. See the handout that is included in this chapter.

Bring in a selection of reference books from each of the categories which are listed on the handout. Keep the sources grouped together just as they appear on the handout, arrange the books on several book carts around the room. Using several carts allows easy access by more than one group at a time.

Enlist the help of another librarian or library assistant who is familiar with the web and can help students stay on track.

Turn on all the computers, bookmarking the following sites:
> http://altavista.digital.com—(Alta Vista)
> http://www.yahoo.com—(Yahoo)
> http://www.occ.com—(online career center)
> http://www.cweb.com—(career web)
> http://www.ceweekly.wa.com/grw.html—(effective resumes)
> http://www.careers.org—(career Net)

PART 2 PRESENTATION: (60 minutes)

- Brief introductory remarks welcoming the students to the library and giving them an overview of the kinds of services that are available to them.

- The librarian spends about five minutes going over the handouts. By focusing on the questions that they should be able to answer at the end of the session, the students can see the format that they will be expected to follow. (5 minutes)

- The librarian then walks around the room, stopping at each of the book carts, highlighting the kind of information they can expect to find in each group of books. By having the librarian walk around the room, the students seem to follow the discussion better than if all the presentation had been from the front of the room. This method brings instruction closer to the student, therefore they feel they are a part of the discussion and often will ask more questions. (10 minutes)

- All the students are then asked to face their computers to begin the hands-on portion of the demonstration.

- Since many of the students have had minimal experience using the web, we take about 30 minutes to learn how to navigate around the screen, demonstrate the difference between a search engine like Alta Vista and a directory service such as Yahoo. Take a few minutes to talk about Boolean operators and their importance in web searching. (30 minutes)

- Visit the four sites that we have bookmarked. As we visit each of the sites, we talk about evaluation techniques to determine the value of each of the sites, always reminding the students how the printed sources compare. (15 minutes)

Hands on Activity: (45 minutes)

- Divide the students into groups of two to three students each, depending on the class size. Each group will be responsible for answering one of the questions in the handouts by using both a printed source and a web source. (25 minutes)

- Each group shares its experiences with the rest of the class, comparing ease of access and the value of their information. (20 minutes)

- The students have the last hour of the class to practice on the web, either looking at sites that are on their handouts or finding their own. (one hour)

Career Research Exercise

Each group is assigned only one question, however everyone receives a copy of the complete exercise so you can take notes when each group shares its experiences.

Step 1   You have at least two more years of school left, maybe more, depending on your career choice. Find a source that will help you finance your education.

A print source:

_____

_____

A web source:

_____

_____

Step 2   Find a school in Florida that offers a bachelor's degree in Public Relations.

A print source:

_____

_____

A web source:

_____

_____

Step 3   What salary can I expect to earn with an electrical engineering degree?

A print source:

_____

_____

A web source:

_____

_____

Step 4   Find a sample resume that you would like to use as your model.

A print source:

_____

A web source:

_____

_____

Step 5   Name a company that offers internships to students majoring in art.

A print source:

_____

_____

A web source:

_____

_____

Step 6   Find a job advertisement for a flower arranger and make a copy of it. Attach it to this sheet.

A print source:

_____

_____

A web source:

_____

_____

Step 7   You have found an ad for a job with The Limited@. Find some information about the company that would give you reason to want to work for them and either copy it or attach it to this sheet.

A print source:

_____

_____

A web source:

_____

_____

Step 8   What kind of public transportation can you find in Boston?

A print source

_____

_____

A web source:

_____

_____

Career Exploration and Development
DOING YOUR RESEARCH IN PRINT SOURCES [Library of Congress call numbers]

Where can I find out about careers?
·*Dictionary of occupational titles*, 4th ed.
    Ref. HB 2595 .U543 1991
·*Encyclopedia of careers and vocational guidance*
    Ref. HF 5381 .E52 1993
·*Occupational outlook handbook*
    Ref. HD 8051 .A62 1996-97
·*Professional careers sourcebook; an information guide for career planning*
    Ref. HF 5382.5 .U5 P76 1990

Which schools offer the programs I need?
·*The college blue book; degrees offered by college and subject.*
    Ref. LA 226 .C685 1995 v.3
·*Index of majors and graduate degrees.*
    Ref. L 901 .C74 1996

How will I be able to finance my education?
·*Chronicle financial aid guide*
    Ref. LB 2337.4 .C47 1992-93
·*The college blue book; scholarships, fellowships, grants and loans.*
    Ref. LA 226 .C685 1995 v.5
·*Directory of financial aids for women 1993-1995.*
    Ref. LB 2338 .D564 1993-95
·*The grants register 1993-95*
    Ref. LB 2338 .G7 1993-95
·*Peterson's paying less for college, 13th ed.*
    Ref. LB 2337.2 .C65 1996
·*Scholarships, fellowships and loans, 11th ed.*
    Ref. LB 2338 .S 1995

Where can I get some experience before I graduate?
·*Peterson's internships 1996*
    Ref. HD 5715.1 I6 1996

How do I write a resume?
·*The overnight resume*
    HD 5383 .A84 1990

Where do I look for a job?

·*Job hunter's yellow pages; the national directory of employment services.*
   Ref. HF 5382.75 .U6 J67 1994
·*Job hunter's sourcebook; where to find employment leads and other job search resources.*
   Ref. HF 5382.75 .U6 J63 1991
·*Non-profits job finder*
   Ref. HD 5710.5 .L38 1992
·*Professional's job finder*
   Ref. HF 5382.75 .U6 L33 1992

What do I know about the companies that are hiring?

·*Companies that care; the most family-friendly companies in America - what they offer and how they got that way.*
   Ref. HF 5549.5 .D39 M67 1991
·*The job seeker's guide to socially responsible companies*
   Ref. HF 5382.75 .U6 J36 1995
·*The 100 best companies for gay men and lesbians*
   Ref. HF 5382 .M48 1994
·*Peterson's job opportunities for engineering, science & computer graduates, 12th ed.*
   Ref. HF 5381 .P48 1991

What happens if I have to relocate for a job?

·*American small city profiles*
   Ref. HT 123 .A6653 1993
·*Cities of the United States*
   Ref. HT 108 .C5 1990
·*The lifestyle market analyst*
   Ref. HF 5415.33 .U6 L54 1990
·*Places rated almanac; your guide to finding the best places to live in America.*
   Ref. HN 60 .B69 1989

Career Exploration and Development
DOING YOUR RESEARCH ON THE WEB

Where can I find out about careers?

http://www.occ.com—(Online Career Center)

http://www.cweb.com—(Career Web)

http://www.careers.org—(Career Net)

http://mapping-your-future.org

Which schools offer the programs I need?

http://www.petersons.com

How will I be able to finance my education?

http://www.finaid.org

http://www.salliemae.com/consumer

http://www.ed.gov/money.html

http://www.internetworld.com/current/feature1.html

Where can I get some experience before I graduate?

http://www.review.com

http://www.jobweb.com/catapult/jintern.htm

http://www.internships.com

http://www.butler.edu/www/career/intern/links.html

How do I write a resume?

http://www.ceweekly.wa.com/grw.html

http://www.careermosaic.com

http://www.vinu.edu/employ4.htm

Where do I look for a job?

http://careerpath.com

http://www.espan.com

http://www1.monster.com:80

http://jobbankusa.com/infoform.html

http://www.ajb.dni.us

http://bestjobsusa.com

What do I know about the companies that are hiring?

http://www.netpart.com/company/search.html

http://www.usc.edu/dept/webster/prospect.htm

What happens if I have to relocate for a job?

http://www.city.net

Relocation salary calculator web site:

http://www.homefair.com/homefair/cmr/salcalc.html

Notes:

JOB SEARCHING ON THE INTERNET

KATHERINE C. EHRLICH

Information Researcher
ERNST & YOUNG, LLP, CLEVELAND, OH

Circumstances for the Instruction Session:

This class is intended for seniors who are graduating and in search of post-schooling opportunities. It is anticipated that students would work independently during free periods or after classes on their own after two initial "in-class" training sessions. Each session lasts approximately 50 minutes.

Objectives of the Instruction:

- To assist graduating students in analyzing their strengths to determine suitable job opportunities.
- To present graduating students with basic guidelines needed in the preparation of a resume.
- To enable graduating students to more easily identify career / job opportunities via use of the Internet.

Components of the Instruction:

Part 1 Preparation
- Selection of Internet sites—several are identified on Exhibit D, or use familiar sites.
- Categorize Sites
    Local
    Regional
    Government / private
- Copy handout for describing ideal job (Exhibit A).
- Copy handout for assessing personal experience (Exhibit B).
- Copy handout of guidelines for drafting a resume (Exhibit C).
- Copy handout describing Internet sites (Exhibit D).

PART 2 CLASSROOM PORTION

SESSION I
- Have students write a description of the ideal job they would like to have.
- Have students assess their personal qualities, abilities, experience; students should be encouraged to work in groups so they can share ideas.
    Students should prepare an individual inventory chart to help them determine exactly what their qualifications and interests are.

Components of the inventory include:
    Work History
    Skills and abilities
    Education
    Interests and talents
    Career goals
    Jobs they want

- After the students have completed the inventory of their personal experience and abilities, have them reassess the job they seek compared to their background. Resources such as *Occupational Outlook Handbook* can be examined by the students to review job title responsibilities and educational and experience requirements of various positions.

SESSION II
- Have students draft a resume using the guidelines of Exhibit C.
- Review basic competencies using windows / mouse environment, and general. searching methodology for the Internet (Yahoo, Lycos, Alta Vista).

Hands-on Portion of Instruction:

- Have students log onto the Internet and visit sites.
- Students should be instructed to review job listings as they relate to their ideal job, and their personal qualification outlined on the inventory. They can then identify logical potential opportunities and develop a list.
- Explain to students how they can evaluate opportunities offered and eliminate / prioritize the jobs which interest them.

Evaluation of the Session: (Exhibit E)

- Evaluate expectations.
- Was the Internet a useful tool for job search?
- Likelihood of reimbursement for relocation if a job was found?
- Timeliness of postings?
- Variety of opportunities?
- How to compare success ratio with local paper offerings?

EXHIBIT A
MY IDEAL JOB

My ideal job would be _____

My job responsibilities would include:

1._____

2._____

3._____

4._____

5.

_____

My job would require that I work _____ hours per day / week, and those hours

would be daytime / evening. I only want to work Monday through Friday. However,

some weekend work hours would be okay. I would / would not be willing to work

overtime.

My minimum acceptable salary is $_____ per hour / week / month.

EXHIBIT B

ASSESSING PERSONAL EXPERIENCE

WORK HISTORY:
List all work experience you have had. Include part-time employment, summer jobs, volunteer work and any internships.

List your job title and describe in detail the duties of each position.
Provide the dates you held each position.
List any special accomplishments.

_____

_____

_____

_____

_____

_____

_____

_____

_____

_____

SKILLS
List and describe any technical skills.

What machinery or equipment can you operate?_____

_____

What computer skills do you have?_____

_____

_____

What foreign language skills do you have?_____

_____

What personal qualities do you have that might make you good at certain jobs? These might be such things as attention to detail, good organizational skills, working well with other people, or being creative.

_____

_____

_____

Education:
List schools attended and degrees earned. Consider which courses you liked the best and why they were favorites. Also list any awards or recognition received.

_____

_____

List any extracurricular activities you have participated in which might have provided experience for a related job._____

_____

_____

Interests and Aptitudes:
Can any of your special talents translate into a job opportunity—fixing cars, drawing well, playing a musical instrument?_____

_____

_____

Career Goals:

How will what you are looking for now prepare you for your long term career-goal, or are you just willing to accept anything for

now?_____

_____

_____

_____

Based on your responses, describe the type of job you want.
List the types of job you are either best qualified for or want; prioritize them.

_____

_____

_____

_____

Is further training or professional schooling required? Do the answers to these questions match the needs of your "ideal job?"

_____

_____

_____

_____

EXHIBIT C

Drafting A Good Resume

DO

Make it easy to read
Be concise
Use language relevant to the job field
Resumes should be no longer than 1–2 pages
Focus should be on accomplishments, not duties
Use "action" verbs rather than pronouns
Proofread for typing errors
Be sure it looks neat

DO NOT

Include reasons for leaving a position and the salary
Include a photograph
Include personal references
Include non-business related hobbies
Include inaccurate information

Elements of a Resume

Personal Data: Name, home mailing address, and telephone numbers.

Job Objective: A simple statement indicating the type of work you are looking for. Don't be so specific that you unnecessarily limit yourself, especially if you are just starting out in a field.

Work History: List your work experience in reverse chronological order. For each position include the following.

    Job Title
    Name, city and state of employer
    Dates of employment (month and year)
    Job description (briefly but specifically describe what you did, citing
facts   and figures of accomplishments where possible.)

Education: List most recent first and work backwards including degrees and diplomas earned, relevant special seminars and training.

Military Experience: List branch and length of service and any major duties related to the job you are seeking.

Miscellaneous: Membership in professional organizations, any articles published, or other unique events.

EXHIBIT D

INTERNET SITES

Yahoo—One of the most popular WWW search engines and one which includes extensive subject menus.

> http://www.yahoo.com

Alta Vista—Considered the largest of the web search databases.

> http://www.altavista.digital.com

Lycos—Good coverage of ftp, and newsgroups, as well as web pages. It has a link to employment opportunities in Finance & Administration, Sales, Marketing, and Administration.

> http://www.lycos.com/lycosinc/lycosjob.html

Online Career Center—This includes keyword searching for all jobs and jobs by city, a place for posting resumes, a link to career fairs, and links for recruiters.

> http://www.occ.com

IntelliMatch—Contains a listing of "Hot Jobs" and "Employer Profiles," as well as a listing of job seekers.

> http://www.intellimatch.com

Nation Job Network—A service listing jobs from across the United States but primarily from the midwest.

> http://www.nationjob.com

The Internet Job Locator—Allows job searching by state, city and job category, and provides connections to other job-search engines.

> http://www.joblocator.com/jobs/

JobWeb—Employment sites are organized by field, and information about employers' internships and relocation resources is available.

> http://www.jobweb.org

Recruitment on-Line—In addition to searching available job postings, a company of the week is highlighted, and there is a link to Employment Agency Listings.

> http://www.helpwanted.com

Career Path—An electronic version of the help-wanted ads from six major newspapers: *The Los Angeles Times; The New York Times; The Chicago Tribune; The Washington Post,* and *The Boston Globe.* Keyword searching is available.

> http://www.careerpath.com

Federal Jobs Database—This is a listing of open positions in the Federal Government. It can be searched by type of job and state.

> http://www.jobweb.org/fedjobsr.htm

FedWorld Vacancies—Listing of Federal government job openings. It is updated daily except for Sundays and Mondays.

> http://www.fedworld.gov/jobs/jobsearch.html

EXHIBIT E

SESSION EVALUATION

1. I expected my search for a job on the Internet to result in: (circle one)

   20 + leads   10—20 leads   0—10 leads

   The search actually resulted in _____ leads

2. I was satisfied with the type of jobs advertised as far as they matched my qualifications.
   _____strongly agree
   _____somewhat agree
   _____agree
   _____disagree
   _____strongly disagree

3. The variety of advertised jobs matched my expectations.
   _____strongly agree
   _____somewhat agree
   _____agree
   _____disagree
   _____strongly disagree

4. It was clear whether or not advertised positions would pay for relocation.
   _____strongly agree
   _____somewhat agree
   _____agree
   _____disagree
   _____strongly disagree

5. The postings appeared to be current and out-dated ones removed from the listings in a timely manner.
   _____strongly agree
   _____somewhat agree
   _____agree
   _____disagree
   _____strongly disagree

6. I believe this was a worthwhile use of job searching time.
   _____strongly agree
   _____somewhat agree
   _____agree
   _____disagree
   _____strongly disagree

7. Have you also pursued jobs advertised in the local newspaper?
   If yes, how does the Internet compare?
   _____ Favorably _____ Unfavorably

8. Did you find government sponsored or private vendor sites more user friendly and more useful?

   Government Site: Relevant jobs _____ Yes _____ No
                        Job variety   _____ Yes _____ No
                        User-friendly _____ Yes _____ No

   Private vendor: Relevant jobs _____ Yes _____ No
                        Job variety   _____ Yes _____ No
                        User-friendly _____ Yes _____ No

9. Did you make any actual contact with potential employers advertising jobs on the Internet?
   _____ Yes
   _____ No
   _____ Tried but unsuccessful
   _____ Awaiting response
   _____ Intend to contact but haven't yet

10. Which search engine (Yahoo, Lycos, Alta Vista, other) did you find most user-friendly when you searched job leads via keyword?

   _____ Yahoo
   _____ Lycos
   _____ Alta Vista
   _____ Other(identify)

   _____
   _____
   _____

SAMPLE SEARCH

1. **What type of job do I want to find** ?

    An accounting job in Austin, Texas

2. **How can I locate job listings on the Internet** ?
   * Log onto the Internet by entering your identification name or number and your password.
   * Use a search engine such as Alta Vista by typing an address,
        http://www.altavista.digital.com
   * Click in the query box, and type "employment."
   * Click on the "submit" button to perform the search.
   * Use the scroll bar to scan the sites retrieved. The first 10 retrieved documents will be listed. To view additional retrieved documents, click on "p. 2" at the bottom of the screen.

3. **Click on the site of most interest to you** .
   * You can click on the words in the title of the site, or on the address.
        "Longhorn Employment Services" or
        http://www.longhornjobs.com
   * Click on the highlighted words "**job list**" on the Longhorn Employment Services home page.
   * Click on the category representing the job you are seeking.
        Bookkeeping / Accounting
   * Read the jobs described. Click on the highlighted words "**Top of Page**" which will provide a link to "**register with Longhorn Employment Services.**" Click on that to register. Instructions for submitting a resume to Longhorn Employment Services will appear.

4. **Click on the "Back" button** .
   * This will return you to the listing of sites retrieved by your "employment" search via Alta Vista.
   * Visit another site for additional job listings.

STUDENT WORK SHEET

What type of job do I want to find?

_____

_____

_____

_____

How can I locate job listings on the Internet?

    Logging on: ID_____ Password _____

    Search engines:

        Alta Vista:_____

        Yahoo:_____

        Others:_____

        _____

        _____

        _____

        _____

Children's Literature on the Net; Spinning a Web of Information

RU STORY-HUFFMAN
Public Services Librarian
CUMBERLAND COLLEGE, WILLIAMSBURG, KY

Circumstances for the Instruction Session:

This presentation was originally prepared as a workshop for practicing educators, and has been adapted for use in an undergraduate academic setting. The 50-minute instructional program is designed for the academic librarian to present to a children's literature class for elementary education majors.

The library instruction session will emphasize the variety of information pertaining to children's literature which can be found on the World Wide Web. As with any group, the experience levels of the participants will vary. It may be necessary to establish proficiency levels of the students before this unit is undertaken. Information will be presented in a format which can be adapted by the students for use in an actual classroom setting.

The format for this lesson can also be adapted to the chapter by Mary Ellen Collins titled "Meeting the Author: Biographical and Critical Resources of Children's Literature." This chapter can be found in *Empowering Students; Hands-on Library Instruction Activities*, (Library Instruction Publications, 1996). With a few revisions, and prior research by the librarian, students can search the Internet to complete the Library Exercises included in Collins' chapter.

Objectives of the Instruction:

- To provide a list of Internet resources on children's literature which can be used in an elementary classroom.
- To provide college students the opportunity to explore the Internet using a subject pertaining to their major field of study.
- To go beyond the "traditional" method of lecture instruction.

Components of the Library Instruction:

PREPARATION:

1. Before attempting this presentation, it is necessary to do research on the Internet. Often, as we all know, a Web site on the Internet can be here today, and gone the next. For this reason, general subject areas have been chosen and only established web pages have been included.

2. Compilation of a bibliography of children's literature web sites, and a general introduction to the Internet can be an added tool.

3. Since actual Internet searching will be done in the session, it is necessary to conduct the sessions in an electronic classroom or academic computing lab. Dependent upon the number of computer terminals available, you may need to split the class into smaller components. Communication with the classroom instructor is vital to establish the size of the classes and level of computer experience.

CLASSROOM PRESENTATION AND HANDS-ON ACTIVITY

1. The students have probably been studying children's literature through the traditional "lecture" method, as well as locating research resources in the traditional way. Explain to them that in this session they will learn a new way to study aspects of children's literature through the Internet. When used as an accompaniment to the traditional lecture, the Internet session can enhance the learning process.

   Spend a few minutes giving a quick overview of the various Internet search engines and evaluation criteria of Internet sites.

   Refer to the chapters on evaluation of Internet resources elsewhere in this volume to aid further in development of lesson plans. The chapter entitled "Teaching World Wide Web Navigation to Small Groups..." includes a page called **WWW Site Evaluation Checklist** which can be copied or adapted as a handout.

2. Using the keyword search term "children's literature," instruct students to begin a search.

3. As the results appear, predetermined sites selected by the librarian can be explored during the class period.

4. If time allows, encourage students to search on their own. Using keyword searches of a more specific nature, students will have the opportunity to expand their knowledge base of children's literature and search skills.

5. Provide students with follow-up hands-on assignments in which they are to search the Internet for information on a topic of their choice in children's literature.

Suggestions for keyword searches to use in this lesson:

- children's literature
- children's authors
- children's illustrators
- children's literature review and criticism
- writing for children
- specific titles of children's books
- publishing and children's books

As students become more proficient in searching, more complex searches can be structured. It is essential that they read the searching instructions which are given by each search engine in order to perform successful searches.

Variations for the Session:

This instruction session was presented as a workshop for a group of educators. Suggestions for variation include expansion of the presentation to cover two class periods, evaluation criteria of web sites, and continual updating of information. Integration of this lesson plan into existing class structure is a possibility for the future.

A SELECTION OF INTERNET SITES FOR CHILDREN'S LITERATURE

Children's Literature Web Guide
http://www.ucalgary.ca/'dkbrown/
> A guide to Internet resources related to children's literature. Provides a variety of information.

Child Study Children's Book Committee
http://www.bnkst.edu
> A presentation of the Child Study Children's Book Committee at Bank Street College.

CBC Online
http://www.cbcbooks.org
> Includes information from the Children's Book Council.

Children's Literature Reference
http://www.lib.utexas.edu/Libs/PCL/child/
> Includes links for Awards and Honor, Classics, Authors and Illustrators, Genre, Reviews and Criticism.

ALSC
http://www.ala.org/alsc.html
> An organization of the American Library Association specializing in library services for children.

AskEric Infoguides: Children's Literature
http://ericir.syr.edu/cgi-bin/markup_infoguides/children_literature
> Information from the ERIC clearinghouse for educational information.

The Internet Public Library
http://www.ipl.org
> Includes a section for children's literature.

Children's Literature Homepage
http://www.parentsplace.com/readroom/childnew/index.html
> A newsletter for adults from ParentsPlace.com, an Internet parenting resource site.

Vandergrift's Children's Literature Page
http://www.scils.rutgers.edu/special/kay/childlit.html
> From Kay E. Vandergrift at Rutgers University.

Exploring Children's Literature Topics on the World Wide Web—Research Assignment 1

Using your favorite search engine, begin a search on a topic of your choice in children's literature. Possible topics can include your favorite children's author or illustrator, classic children's literature, the history of children's literature or review and criticism of children's literature. The components of your searching assignment are included below.

Topic _____

List the keywords you will use:

1st choice_____

2nd choice_____

3rd choice_____

Search engine used to search 1st choice

_____

Number of sites or "hits"

_____

Link chosen to explore

_____

What is the format of this link? Is it:

a list of further links _____ a newsletter _____

personal homepage _____ organizational page _____

other _____

What is the scope of this link?

Educational _____

Fun _____

Informational _____

Other _____

_____

Who produced this link?

_____

_____

Are there links to other Internet sites included? If so, what are they?

_____

_____

_____

_____

What information did you gain from this Internet site?

_____

_____

_____

How would you use this Internet site in an educational setting?

_____

_____

_____

List strengths and weaknesses of this Internet site.

_____

_____

_____

_____

_____

Would you recommend this site to other educators? Discuss why or why not.

_____

_____

_____

_____

_____

_____

Comparing "Search Engines"—Research Assignment 2

In this assignment you will compare and contrast various Internet search engines. Choose 1 topic and conduct a search on that topic using 3 different search engines. Complete the assignment using the knowledge you gained in Research Assignment 1.

Topic _____

Search Engines used:

1. _____

2. _____

3. _____

Number of Hits in each, respectively:

1. _____

2. _____

3. _____

Using the first 10 hits, are there any links which appear using all 3 search engines? If so, what are they?

_____

_____

_____

Which search engine provided the most useful hits? Discuss why.

_____

_____

_____

_____

What is different about the 3 search engines?

_____

_____

_____

_____

_____

_____

What is similar about the search engines?

_____

_____

_____

_____

_____

_____

Which search engine do you like best? Discuss why.

_____

_____

_____

_____

_____

_____

_____

Be prepared to discuss and share your findings in class.

ERIC Research Techniques for Web-Based Searching

EMALY CONERLY
Assistant Department Head of Circulation
FLORIDA STATE UNIVERSITY, TALLAHASSEE

THURA R. MACK
Assistant Professor/Reference Librarian
UNIVERSITY OF TENNESSEE-KNOXVILLE

Circumstances for the Instruction Session:

In the spring of 1997, the University of Tennessee-Knoxville Libraries moved to a web-based format of on-line databases that are accessible to UTK students, faculty, and staff through the UTK library's world wide web homepage.

ERIC is one of the databases most heavily used by Education faculty and students. The UTK College of Education is a strong research oriented department with many ongoing research projects and activities. Therefore, this research and library instruction guide is designed to aid students and other researchers in effectively accessing information on a wide variety of education topics and issues. The majority of the users are graduate students and teaching faculty. However, the instructions and activities outlined in this chapter can be used by a number of other users outside the education field, from the beginners to the highly skilled ones. Some guiding principles behind this library instruction chapter are as follows:

- Education students are required to conduct research toward a written research report.
- The library component is provided to introduce students to research sources and skills.
- The library class session and accompanying assignments are developed after an interview with the professor to access the information/research needs of the class.
- Many of these search techniques can be used for searching other available databases.

Objectives of Instruction:

- to review how to develop a search strategy, using Boolean logic and/or truncation
- to introduce the World Wide Web, including:
    a. basic Web terminology ("Glossary" handout)
    b. Navigational tools and features of Web browser selected Web search engines
    c. Electronic style manual sites (Style manual handout) for citing Web documents/resources

- to demonstrate searching techniques for the Web-based ERIC database.
- to provide hands-on activities in which students search a certain topic on the Web and in ERIC, report the results of that search, and give a bibliographic citation for a selected record.

Components of Instruction

PART 1 PREPARATION

- Communication with the instructor:
  - Specific information needed to be covered in class
  - Date of class
  - Time of class
  - Library location for class session
  - Number of students in order to prepare handouts

- Reserve Infotech Lab or library instruction room and workstations in Reference

- Before class, select relevant topics to search during demonstration, prepare handouts, and place handouts at each workstation.

PART 2 PRESENTATION

- Welcome
- Introduce yourself
- Explain goal of the library instruction class and what will be covered
- Review handouts
- Provide overview of library layout, with an emphasis on public services, and computer access locations
- Demonstration of:
  - how to develop a search strategy
  - how to use a Web browser and search the Web
  - where to find style manuals for citing electronic resources, and
  - how to search ERIC

The session lasts for 90 minutes. It generally consists of about 25 students from the College of Education, primarily graduate or intern students. The library instructor gives a one hour presentation/demonstration tailored to meet the research interests of the individual class. Thirty minutes are allocated for students to begin hands-on activities; they work in groups of three.

Hands-on Activities:

- Divide students into groups of three.
- Use library research exercise designed for this class.
- Each student will select a subject or topic to use in the library research exercise.
- Each student should get the opportunity to perform an on-line search.
- Students should be encouraged to find specific information on their chosen topics to provide more stimulation as they go through the library research exercise.
- Remind students that it is essential to keep printouts for bibliographic citations and documentation.

Follow-up:

Remind students that ERIC journal records begin with accession number EJ and document records begin with accession number ED. To locate these items, logout of the ERIC database first and then check the library's on-line catalog. ERIC documents will be located in the Documents/Microforms Department on micro-fiche. Journals owned by the UTK library will either be in the stacks by call number or on microfilm.

Evaluation:

The librarian needs to check with each group as it works in the library to ascertain how it is functioning. Specifically:

- Check to see if instructions are clear.
- Ask students how their search is progressing.
- Determine if there are problems retrieving desired information.
- Ask the professor if instructional content was adequate, relevant, and effective.
- Provide e-mail address of the librarians involved in the session for those who wish to follow-up with questions and further assistance.

ERIC RESEARCH TECHNIQUES EXERCISES

Step 1   **Select one** of the three topics listed below:
- Ebonics—issues, problems, use
- English as a second language (ESL) for kindergarten students
- reading instruction for hearing-impaired

Step 2   Write out search concepts:

_____

_____

Step 3   Add any limiting factors—date, language, country, age/grade level.

_____

Step 4   Write a search statement using Boolean logic and/or truncation.

_____

_____

_____

Step 5   Using the ERIC database:
a. Perform a basic search.

b. Perform a search using the thesaurus and/or index.

c. Limit search results to the document type—Research-report.

d. What were the results from your search?
Print out one record from your search.

e. Determine if the library has the document for this citation, and write the location of the document. Was the citation an ERIC document or journal?

f. What was needed from the ERIC record to make a bibliographic citation according to APA rules?

_____

g. Did you encounter any difficulties or frustrations in your search?

_____

_____

_____

h. Logout of databases.

Step 6   Find a Web site that relates in some way to your topic.
a. What search strategy did you use to find this site?

_____

_____

b. What is the URL for the site?

_____

c. Print the first page of the site.

d. Give a bibliographic citation for this site, by referring to an electronic style manual.

_____

_____

e. Did you encounter any difficulties or frustrations in your search?

_____

_____

Please hand in this exercise sheet, along with your printouts, to the instructor.

ERIC Research Techniques
for Web-based Searching

ERIC is a major database covering the literature of the education field. It derives its name from the Educational Resources Information Center, a national information network, that is sponsored by the U.S. Department of Education. The Center is comprised of 16 subject-specialized clearinghouses, each collecting education information in their subject areas. For more information on ERIC and the ERIC Clearinghouses, go the World Wide Web site http://aspensys.com/eric/.

The ERIC database indexes and abstracts journal articles, research reports, lesson plans, reference materials, theses, dissertations, etc. The database includes the *Resources in Education (RIE), Current Index to Journals in Education (CIJE),* and 850 *ERIC Digest* records in full-text format.

The University of Tennessee (UT) Web version of the ERIC database has access limited to UT students, faculty, and staff. It is available at http://www.lib.utk.edu—(select "Databases").

Alternative sites that permit unlimited Web access are http://ericir.syr.edu/ at Syracuse University and the US Department of Education site, http://www.ed.gov/pubs/.

PREPARING FOR A SEARCH IN ERIC:

Develop a search statement.
- Identify key concepts of your topic, and
- List any limitations of your topic such as a **certain time period** or **geographic region**, or **language**, or **type of material** such as research reports, lesson plans, etc.

Refine a search or connect key concepts and limitations.
1. **Connect** terms with **Boolean Logic.**

   Boolean Logic is a technique of using the most basic forms of expression to represent any logical possibility. The following are examples of logical operators used in Boolean Logic:

Operator	Search Example	Finds Records Containing
OR	academic **or** achievement	**either** academic **or** achievement
AND	academic **and** achievement	**both** academic **and** achievement
NOT	academic **not** achievement	academic **but not** achievement
OR	retrieves all records that contain at least one of the search terms	
AND	retrieves all records that contain all of the search terms	
NOT	eliminates a search term or group of search terms	

2. Truncation is used to retrieve all forms of a word. Use * key to truncate.
    Teenage* will retrieve teenager, teenagers, teenaged, etc.

3. Parentheses ( ) are used in complex search statements to group terms joined by OR:
    (hazardous or toxic) AND waste*

BEGIN THE SEARCH:

The steps which follow are based on the ERIC site mounted at the University of Tennessee. Other libraries must adapt the steps, if necessary, to their own library homepage or to the sites which were listed in the opening paragraphs of this handout.

1. Begin by going to ERIC on the WWW.

- **Open** Netscape to the UTK Library Homepage http://www.lib.utk.edu/.
- **Select** Databases from the Homepage Menu.
- **Select** "Education" from the subject categories listed.
- **Select** ERIC from Education database menu.
    ERIC opens to the Search Screen:
    1. Type the term or terms in the Search Box. Select **Where** the search terms will be searched (Words Anywhere, Title, etc.), the **Language**, and the **publication years**.
    2. Click the Search button.
    3. The number of records retrieved by the search are displayed on the next Search Screen. You have the choice to modify your search or view your results.

MODIFY THE SEARCH:

A. **COMBINE SEARCHES**:
    1. Use the right-hand scroll bar or the down-arrow key to move to the Search History, located in the lower portion of the Search Screen. Searches are listed in reverse chronological order.
    2. To combine:
        ➢ Click the boxes to the left of the numbered searches.
        ➢ Select either AND (default) or OR to join the searches.
        ➢ Click the **Combined Checked** button.
    3. As an alternative, use the set numbers for completed searches in place of terms in the Search Box:
        Example: communication and #1

B. REFINE SEARCHES:

1. By using the Thesaurus in ERIC:
   The Thesaurus is a list of the defined subject descriptors used in ERIC. This is the most helpful tool in ERIC for subject searching.

   - **Click** on **Thesaurus** at the top of the Search screen.
   - Type in the term that you are searching, such as "content area reading."
   - **Click** the **Jump** button.
     This puts you into a Thesaurus subject list.
   - **Select** the Hypertext term "content area reading" and click on it.
     This takes you to a screen that gives you the history, definition, and use of the term, with broader, narrower, or related terms. This is very useful in stimulating ideas for searching.
   - **Click** the **Search** button to search this term or **Explode** button to search this term and all of the narrower terms.
   - **Click** on any other Hypertext term on the Thesaurus Term Screen. That takes you to the term detail page for that term.
   - **View** the results after you search a term.

2. By using the **ERIC Index**:
   ERIC has an alphabetical index that records the occurrence of phrases in the material indexed. This is especially helpful for searching for citations by a particular author or in a certain journal or by identifiers (i.e., keywords that are not established as ERIC-approved descriptors).

   - **Click** on Index at top of Screen Menu Screen.
   - **Type** in the author's name or the title of the journal at Index Search Screen.

     Note: Put a "hyphen" between words to create a bound phrase.
Ex: Author:	Kimball-Bruce
Journal title:	Journal-of-Education
Identifier:	Parenting-stress-index

   - In field box, **select Free Text**.
   - **Click Display** button. This takes you into an alphabetical list of words in Index.
   - **Mark** the name or phrase that you want.
   - **Click** the **Search** button.
     This searches the term and you can now choose to view results.

3. By using **Command language** and searching **fields** of the records, you can retrieve:
   INFORMATION BY A PARTICULAR AUTHOR:
   Ex: Kimball in AU

INFORMATION BY DOCUMENT TYPE:

NOTE: Document Types and numbers can be found by clicking Help in the top menu, scrolling down on the Help screen to Help for ERIC. Go to Table of Contents and select Document Types.

SAMPLE DOCUMENT TYPES

041	Dissertations/Theses——Doctoral Dissertations	110	Numeric/Quantitative Data
050	Guides - General	120	Opinion Papers
051	Guides - Classroom - Learner	130	Reference Materials - General
052	Guides - Classroom - Teacher	140	Reports - General
055	Guides - Non-classroom	143	Reports - Research
090	Legal/Legislative/Regulatory Materials	150	Speeches/Meeting papers
100	Non-Print Media	160	Tests/Questionnaires
101	Computer Programs	171	Multilingual/Bilingual Materials

Ex: DTN=143 (for Reports - Research)

INFORMATION FROM A PARTICULAR JOURNAL:

Note: Put a "hyphen" between the words in the title to create a "bound" phrase, Ex: journal-of-education in J N.

VIEW SEARCH RESULTS:

1. To view the results, click on plain Display button next to the number of retrieved records. An ERIC record is then displayed.
    Note: The fields are listed in abbreviated form down the left side of the record. The basic fields are listed below:

AN	Accession Number
AU	Author
TI	Title
PY	Publication Year
JN	Journal Type
DT	Document Type
DE	Descriptors
	DER=minor descriptors
	DEM=major descriptors
AB	Abstract
LA	Language
DTN	Document Type Number

    ➢ For a complete list of fields, click on Help in top menu. At Help screen, scroll down to Help for ERIC. Click on List of Fields.
    ➢ Journal records begin with accession number **EJ** (Ex: EJ427527)
    ➢ Locate journal titles in the online catalog, record call number, and location in the library.
    ➢ Document records begin with accession number **ED** (Ex: ED387498)
    ED records are available on microfiche.

2. Up to 10 records will display on a Search Results screen. Movement to other groups of 10 records can be done by clicking either the **Next 10** or **Previous 10** buttons.
3. **Mark** records for printing, downloading, or mailing by clicking the small box to the upper left of each individual record entry. An "**X**" will appear.
4. To change the viewing format, click the plain **Change Display** button.
5. Select the desired fields or formats by clicking the appropriate box(es), and then click the **Confirm Changes** button.

PRINTING SEARCH RESULTS:

1. To prepare for printing, click the **Print** button on the display screen.
2. **Click** on the appropriate button to indicate the records to be printed:
   - ➢ Records displayed on the previous page
   - ➢ First 10 to 50 records in the current search
   - ➢ Marked records.
3. Notice in the lower section that **Search History** is already marked. This Search History gives you a record of the searches that you have performed.
4. To print, click the **Display for print** button. This will reformat the records to be printed.
5. **Note:** Click the **Print** button on the Web browser to begin printing.

End Search: Logout

Click the Logout button at the top or bottom of the screen when you have finished searching.

Glossary

Terms taken from:
   Stussman, B. (1995) Network terms to get you through the 1990s. *The ERIC Review*, 4(1),12-14.

Communication software—a program you install on your computer to enable it to exchange information with another computer via a modem.

Cyberspace—a term used to explain the theoretical boundaries of the Internet and other online services; coined by William Gibson in his 1984 science fiction novel, *Neuromancer*.

E-mail—electronic mail in which messages are sent through a network. To send e-mail, you need an e-mail address which is a combination of letters, numbers, and symbols you select when you get an account on the Internet or subscribe to a commercial online service.

Hypertext—a way of organizing and linking information that allows users to access related text, images, or sounds from a single computer screen. For example, a user reading an encyclopedia entry on jazz on any hypertext-capable system could also hear excerpts from recordings, look up biographical facts about musicians, and see photos of them. Hypertext is the basis of the World Wide Web.

Hypertext Transfer Protocol (HTTP)—a standard used by World Wide Web servers to provide rules for moving text, images, and sound across the Internet.

Information Superhighway—often used as a synonym for the Internet, this theoretical concept is actually much broader, encompassing cable, video, and other communication channels expected to be linked together in the future and easily accessible from homes, schools, and workplaces.

Internet—a worldwide collection of computer networks that serves as a conduit for the transfer of messages and files. It is operated most commonly from education and research institutions; individuals have accounts on nodes.

National Information Infrastructure (NII)—a broad proposal for the federal government to establish standards and governing bodies for the transmission of digital data. Most provisions of the NII are still being debated. Secretary of Education Richard W. Riley refers to the NII as a "seamless web" of communication networks, computers, databases, telephones, televisions, radios, and satellites.

Network—a group of interconnected computers that can communicate with each other. Computers on a local area network (LAN) are on the same floor or in the same building, are directly connected to a file server, and share equipment such as printers. Wide area networks (WANs) link computers or LANs over a greater distance. Computers may be wired directly or have remote, dial-up access to a network node.

Surfing the 'Net—the act of looking for information on the Internet.

URL—Uniform Resource Locator is an address system for naming World Wide Web locations and materials.

Web browser—a client program that enables users to navigate the graphics-oriented portion of the Internet known as the World Wide Web. Web browsers such as Lynx, Mosaic, and Netscape allow users to take advantage of hypertext links to move from item to item on the Web. Web browsers enable users to access images, text, audio, animation, and specialized scientific data files. (A word of caution: Not everyone on the Internet can access the World Wide Web through Web browsers because their image capabilities require high bandwidth and a fairly sophisticated computer.)

World Wide Web (also called the Web)—a hypertext system for finding and accessing Internet resources organized by colorful, graphics-oriented "home-pages." The Web links objects seamlessly so users can go directly to particular item located anywhere in cyberspace. To access the Web, users need a modem, an Internet connection, and a special client program (see Web browser).

Style Manuals:

American Psychological Association. *Publication Manual of the American Psychological Association*, 3rd ed. Washington, D.C.: American Psychological Association, 1983.

Electronic Style Manual Site:
http://www.lib.utk.edu/refs/styles.html

Notes:

Consumer Health Information on the Internet

ANN PERBOHNER
Information Services Manager
RESEARCH ACCESS, INC., PITTSBURGH, PA

Circumstances for the Instruction Session:

It has been estimated that over 40% of Internet users regularly access health and medical resources. Just as students may require the help of librarians to search for library materials, so too do they need help in choosing good search keywords when using the Internet. This particular instruction session will help students understand the importance of formulating their search queries and evaluating the quality of their results.

These instructions can be successfully used for all levels of users from undergraduates to adult learners.

There are four library exercises, which can be used with small to medium groups of students. For large groups, it is suggested that you have an assistant to help students as they search.

Before using these exercises for your class, check the Yahoo and Alta Vista sites for any operational enhancements they may have added after publication of this book.

Objectives of the Instruction:

- Teach basic concepts of Internet searching
- Introduce concept of different types of search tools
- Introduce concept of evaluating Internet resources
- Provide hands-on activities to find material for the student

Components of the Library Instruction:

PREPARATION:
This instruction session requires that students have prior experience using the Internet browser used in your library or place of instruction. Set up classroom area so your students can easily logon to the Internet. If available, use a computer projection system for demonstration to the class.

PRESENTATION:
- Class length is designed for 50-minutes. If you include the optional modules, the class length should be adjusted or split into two sessions (Directory and Automated web searching) to allow for ample search time.

- **DISCUSS SIMILARITIES OF INTERNET SEARCHING TO LIBRARY ESEARCH**
  What type of information is the student looking for, how will the information be used, and what are they expecting to get out of the search. See the sheet of Search Engine Tips included at the end of the chapter.

Search engine basics.

- *Searching Yahoo*
  Search by subject areas
  Search the entire site
  Advanced searching on Yahoo

  (Optional Module) To introduce the concept of a directory structured Internet search tool, consider using the module *What is a web index?*, from *The 15 Minute Series,* a collaboration of InterNIC and LITA, a division of ALA http://rs.internic.net/nic-support/15min/.

- *Searching Alta Vista*
  Simple search
  Advanced search
  Using Live Topics

  (Optional Module) To introduce the concept of an automated search index, consider using the module *What is a web search engine?*, from *The 15 Minute Series,* a collaboration of InterNIC and LITA, a division of ALA http://rs.internic.net/nic-support/15min/.

- **EVALUATE CONSUMER HEALTH INFORMATION RESULTS**

  Critical evaluation of web-based resources has some similarity to evaluation of print resources. Five areas to be covered are:

  >**Accuracy**—Propaganda Vs. Scholarship, avoiding quacks and watch for red flags
  >**Authority**—qualifications of authors
  >**Objectivity**—reliability
  >**Currency**—maintenance and revision of resource
  >**Coverage**—level of treatment- intended audience
  [See also the chapter in this book by Necia Parker-Gibson entitled "ACRES: Accessibility, Content, Relevance, Effectiveness, and Stability of Internet Sites"]

  Evaluation of web-based medical sources adds additional issues concerning reliability.
  >Are the pages really advertisements?
  >Does the site claim to be the only authority on the topic?
  >Is there an e-mail address or contact information?
  >Is there a fee for information or site access?
  >Who maintains the site, individuals, companies, government, etc.?

>Is the report you found published in a peer-reviewed journal?
>Will this resource be available tomorrow?
>Are there links to other reliable sites?
>Have any Web reviewers given their approval—such as Magellan
http://www.mckinley.com/magellan/Reviews/Health_and_Medicine/index.mag
ellan.html
>Does the web site display Health on the Net Code of Conduct symbol (HONcode)?
Web sites displaying the HONcode state that they provide medical or health
information which meets certain quality standards.
Http://www.hon.ch/HONcode/Conduct.html

Evaluation

- Check the students as they search to determine if the questions are self-explanatory.
- Encourage the students to ask questions as they search.
- Ask the students at the end of class to determine if they were helped by the instruction.
- Review their written answers to determine if the students understood the conceptual difference between Yahoo and Alta Vista.
- Review the written answers to determine if the students understand the importance of evaluating their results.

Hands-on Activities

The practice activities which have been planned for this instruction session are set up separately on the pages which follow.

Remind users that they don't need to limit themselves to the random hit or miss nature of locating medical information on the Internet. The resources listed below will help get them started locating web-based resources for Consumer Health Information:

- Patient Education Material http://members.aol.com/DrsPage/pted.htm
- http://www.yahoo.com/Health—used in this instruction session.
- The Alternative Medicine Homepage http://www.pitt.edu/~cbw/altm.html
- Medline—the premiere index for medical research and literature is available free at several Internet sites. The Medical Matrix at http://www.slackinc.com/matrix/medline.html—one source to locate Medline access.
- Webcrawler http://webcrawler.com/select/med.new.html
- Health on the Net Foundation http://www.hon.ch/
- A consumer health information site from the US government is http://www.healthfinder.gov/

Consumer Health Information; An Internet Searching Exercise Using a Subject Directory

Subject directories like Yahoo use people to classify resources. The categories can be searched but are designed for browsing. The benefit of human intervention adds a high level of sensitivity to the results of your search.

Use http://yahoo.com to find web sites and pages relating to Chronic Fatigue Syndrome (CFS)

USING CATEGORIES WITHIN YAHOO.COM

Step 1   Write down a few keywords or concepts to use as search terms.

_____

_____

Step 2   Logon to yahoo.com and select the *HEALTH* category.

Step 3   Select the subcategory *DISEASES AND CONDITIONS*.

Step 4   Select *CHRONIC FATIGUE SYNDROME*, browse the results and record the total hits.

_____

Searching Yahoo.com

Step 5   From Yahoo's homepage, type *CHRONIC FATIGUE SYNDROME* in the search box.

Step 6   What is the difference in your search results when you search across the Yahoo site vs. going directly to the Chronic Fatigue Syndrome sub category?

_____

_____

Step 7 From the Health category, search within this area only and compare your results.

_____

_____

Step 8 Experiment with using alternate search terms such as *CFS,* and compare your results.

_____

_____

Step 9 After locating a site of interest to you, write down several ways you can locate this Internet site again.

_____

_____

Step 10 Evaluate this site as an appropriate resource.
         What are you looking at to determine if this site is a valuable medical resource?

_____

_____

_____

Step 11 Locate and write down the address of the CFIDS Association.

_____

Step 12 Evaluate Yahoo as a tool for finding information about CFS.

_____

_____

_____

_____

_____

Consumer Health Information; An Internet Searching Exercise Using an Automated Search Index

Alta Vista uses "robots" to automatically collect titles, links and text from Internet sites. A database is created, indexed and searched by a powerful search engine. With an effective query, you will retrieve results with a high precision.

Use http://altavista.digital.com to find web sites and pages relating to Chronic Fatigue Syndrome (CFS)

Step 1 Write down a few keywords or concepts you can use as search terms.

_____

_____

Step 2 Look at the opening choices on Alta Vista before entering your first search for _CHRONIC FATIGUE SYNDROME._ The default search screen is for a _Simple Query._ Choose the _standard form_ for results while searching the web.

Step 3 Note the type of results and record the number of hits.

_____

Step 4 Enter the search phrase "CHRONIC FATIGUE SYNDROME" and browse your results.

Step 5 Enter the search +CHRONIC +FATIGUE +SYNDROME and compare with previous results.

_____

Step 6 Choose another search such as _CFS_ and use _LIVE TOPICS_ to narrow your search.

Step 7 What is the difference in the search process using Yahoo and Alta Vista?

_____

_____

_____

Step 8 After locating a site of interest to you, write down several ways you can use to locate this Internet site again.

_____

_____

Step 9 Evaluate this site as an appropriate resource. What are you looking at to determine if this site is a valuable medical resource?

_____

_____

Step 10 Describe the difference between the results you obtain searching for CFS on Yahoo and Alta Vista.

_____

_____

Step 11 Find the CFS FAQ (Frequently Asked Questions) and write the steps you took to locate this resource.

_____

_____

Step 12 Evaluate Alta Vista as tool for locating information about CFS.

_____

_____

Consumer Health Information; An Internet Searching Exercise Using a Subject Directory for a Topic of your Choice

Use Yahoo.com *to find web sites and pages relating to your chosen health topic*

Using categories within Yahoo.com

Step 1   Write down a few keywords or concepts you can use as search terms.

_____

_____

Step 2   Logon to Yahoo.com and select the *HEALTH* category.

Step 3   Select the subcategory *DISEASES AND CONDITIONS, or a category that matches your topic.*

_____

Step 4   Select and browse the results.

Searching Yahoo.com

Step 5   Within Yahoo's home page, type *YOUR SEARCH HERE* in the search box.

Step 6   What is the difference in your search results when you search across the Yahoo site vs. going directly to a sub category?

_____

_____

_____

Step 7   From the Health category, select search within this area only, and compare your results.

_____

_____

_____

Step 8   Experiment with using alternate search terms, and compare your results.

_____

_____

_____

_____

Step 9   After locating a site of interest to you, write several ways you can locate this Internet site again.

_____

_____

_____

Step 10 Evaluate this site as an appropriate resource. What are you looking at to determine if this site is a valuable health resource?

_____

_____

_____

_____

Step 11 Can you locate an association related to your search topic? Write down the address or other contact information for your search topic.

_____

_____

Consumer Health Information; An Internet Searching Exercise Using an Automated Search Index for a Topic of your Choice

Use http://altavista.digital.com to find web sites and pages relating to your chosen health topic

Step 1 Write down a few keywords or concepts you can use as search terms for a topic of your choice.

_____

_____

_____

Step 2 Look at the opening choices on Alta Vista before entering your first search for *your keywords here*. The default search screen is for a *Simple Query*. Choose the STANDARD FORM for results while searching the web.

Step 3 Note the type of results and record the number of hits.

_____

_____

Step 4 Enter the search phrase "YOUR CHOICE HERE" and browse your results.

_____

Step 5 Enter the search +CHOOSE +YOUR +WORDS +carefully and compare with previous results.

_____

_____

Step 6 Choose another search and use *Live Topics* to narrow your search.

_____

Step 7 After locating a site of interest to you, write down several ways you can use to locate this Internet site again.

_____

_____

Step 8 Evaluate this site as an appropriate resource. What are you looking at to determine if this site is a valuable health resource?

_____

_____

_____

Step 9 Find and record a resource such as an association or point of contact for further information on your topic.

_____

Step 10 Is there a difference in the search process for you when you know the terms to use vs. making up your own?

_____

_____

Step 11 Do you prefer using Yahoo or Alta Vista as a search tool for your topic? Write down your response and include reasons why you would choose one search tool over another for various health topics.

_____

_____

_____

Search Engine Tips

	Alta Vista	Yahoo
Approximate # Web pages indexed	31 Million	250,000
Default simple search	Case sensitive if you use Caps; Exact word search; Logical OR	AND, Wildcard follows every term
Automatic inclusion of alternate search	N/A	Automatically uses Alta Vista to search web if no Yahoo categories or sites are found
Additions to simple search screen	Use * for wildcard; Use " " For phrase searching; Use + preceding word to require it; Use - preceding word to not include it; Use AND, OR, NEAR, AND NOT; Nesting with ( ) Search Web or Usenet	Use " " For phrase searching; Use + preceding word to require it; Use - preceding word to not include it
Advanced search	Filter by date; Keyword weighting	Use Options button for: Switch to OR; Substring or Complete word search; Set # of hits; Filter by date; Search for URL; Search Usenet or e-mail address
Fields Indexed	Title; text; URL; Other	URL Title Comment
Help	Yes, available for simple and advanced queries	http://www.yahoo.com/docs/info/help.html
Criteria for URL inclusion	Robots comb the web	User submission, Robots look for new web announcements
Updates	Combs the web in 4-6 weeks	Daily updates
Strength	Large; Indexes every word	Well-organized; Organized by humans; Good place to start
Weakness	Difficult to narrow search	Not comprehensive

Psychology Research; A Roadmap for Utilizing the Internet

Elizabeth W. Carter

Assistant Professor and Information Services Librarian
The Citadel, Charleston, SC

Linda Ross

Instructor, Psychology Department
The Citadel, Charleston, SC

Circumstances for the Instruction Sessions:

College librarians are constantly working with students and faculty who want to use the Internet in research. As more and more information comes online, the Internet has become a popular extension of more traditional sources of library research. Just as students require instruction to effectively use catalogs, periodical indexes, and other library resources, both print and online, they need to be taught to utilize Internet resources effectively and appropriately.

This chapter provides a series of instructional exercises designed to introduce Internet searching techniques; it can be used in its entirety, or individual exercises can stand alone to illustrate a specific aspect of Internet searching. All instruction can fit into one class period, allowing students to continue assignments on their own, or may be covered over several class periods with work done in class.

The instruction is designed to enable undergraduate and graduate students to incorporate the Internet into psychology research by suggesting strategies to effectively locate, use, and evaluate Internet resources.

Student skill level: These exercises assume students have basic Internet navigating skills (i.e., pointing and clicking, navigating forward and back through pages, and printing).

Objectives of the Instruction:

Through a series of library based activities, students will:

1. develop a search strategy for a research hypothesis.
2. learn important terms associated with the Internet.
3. become acquainted with Internet search engines and directories.
4. develop skills to evaluate Internet sites.
5. develop skills to evaluate information found on the Internet.
6. develop an appreciation for the potential of the Internet through virtual libraries.
7. develop an understanding of the state of electronic journals in psychology.

8. learn to properly cite Internet sources.
9. develop an understanding of the role of the Internet in psychology research.

Components of the Instruction:

This class is team taught by a librarian and psychology instructor. The librarian teaches the skills to search and access Internet sources; the psychology instructor teaches students assessment techniques and provides context and guidance in incorporating sources into research projects.

The class should be held in a computer lab providing a computer and projection capability for the instructor and hands-on access for students.

Exercise 1   Develop a search strategy
Exercise 2   Internet terminology
Exercise 3   Using Internet search engines and directories
Exercise 4   Evaluate Internet sites
Exercise 5   Evaluate Internet information
Exercise 6   Virtual libraries
Exercise 7   Electronic journals in psychology
Exercise 8   Citing electronic sources

Evaluation:

To assess effectiveness, a survey is included for students to complete at unit's end. The survey is designed to assist instructors on measuring whether instructional objectives have been achieved. This ten item, five point Likert scale survey may be used to assess the effectiveness of library instruction in teaching students to effectively use the Internet as a research tool in psychology. The survey asks students to rate their level of agreement with statements about activities and instruction. Survey questions were designed to measure the instructional objectives. Students were requested to check their response on the 1 to 5 scale, with **1 indicating not at all true** and **5 indicating very true.**

___1___2___3___4___5   My ability to use the Internet improved through this class.
___1___2___3___4___5   The exercises helped me learn to use the Internet.
___1___2___3___4___5   I am better able to incorporate Internet sources into my research after this class.
___1___2___3___4___5   It is important for college students to know how to use the Internet.
___1___2___3___4___5   Librarians were helpful.
___1___2___3___4___5   Instructors effectively explained procedures for the exercises.
___1___2___3___4___5   Library activities provided opportunities to understand the value and limitations of the Internet in scholarly research.
___1___2___3___4___5   Library activities helped me learn to evaluate Internet sites.
___1___2___3___4___5   Library activities helped me learn to evaluate information found on the Internet.
___1___2___3___4___5   Library exercises helped me to understand the role of the Internet in psychology research.

Develop a Search Strategy—Exercise 1

Research in psychology requires a question and use of the empirical method to answer it. Whether a researcher uses print data bases, electronic databases, or Internet sites there are steps to make a search more effective. Research is theory driven; a review of the literature provides an understanding of what has been covered in the area and what questions are being asked.

This activity is designed to help in selection of a topic for a literature review and locating and evaluating relevant information on Internet sites.

Select an independent variable
First, select a topic of interest (for example; **depression in college students**).
Think about this variable.
1. What might cause a person to be in a certain category?
2. What factors may be related to a high score (or a low score) within a category?

Select a dependent variable
Second, select a second variable (for example; **academic achievement**) that may be logically related to the first variable.
Think about both variables.
1. How are they be related?
2. Is there possible cause and effect?
3. How could they be correlated?
4. What would be related to a high (or a low) score?

Operationalize the variables
Define or **operationalize** the variables.

Independent variable:_____
For example, for **depression** use *Beck Depression Inventory*.

Dependent variable:_____
For example, for academic achievement use **grade point average**.

Working hypothesis
Examine the relationship between the independent variable and the dependent variable:

For example,
There may be a relationship between depression in college students and academic achievement.

Search Strategy Worksheet

Working hypothesis:

Database:

Search Terms: (Include any operational definitions or related terms)

Independent variable	Dependent variable
_____	_____

or

| _____ | _____ |

or

_____   AND   _____

Internet Terminology—Exercise 2

The following are important Internet terms and definitions.

Bookmark—A Web browser feature allowing users to "mark" sites to which they would like to return, thereby creating a list of favorite sites.

Gopher (gopher protocol)—Retrieves menus and documents from Gopher servers. Example: gopher://gopher.citadel.edu

FTP (File Transfer Protocol)—Retrieves files from anonymous FTP servers. Example: ftp://ftp2.cc.ukans.edu

Home page (or page)—The main or front page of a Web document.

HTML (HyperText Markup Language)—Codes which create hypertext links between documents.

HTTP (Hyper-Text Transfer Protocol)—Retrieves hypertext (HTML) documents and other items from Web servers. Example: http://www.citadel.edu

Hypertext—A collection of related documents with "links" between documents. In hypertext documents, links or "hot" items (usually in bold or otherwise denoted from the rest of the text). When selected, these links allow users to view the related document.

Internet directory—A collection of Internet resources combining control of virtual libraries with comprehensiveness of search engines (such as Yahoo). See Exercise 3 for descriptions of specific search engines and Internet directories.

Protocol—The kind of communications required to retrieve files.

Search engine—Also called Internet search tools, these are programs which provide keyword searching of the Internet. See Exercise 3 for descriptions of specific search engines and Internet directories (such as *Alta Vista, Lycos, InfoSeek* and *WebCrawler*).

Toolbar—Row of "buttons" displayed in Web browsers allowing users to move **forward**, go **back**, return **home**, and **print**.

URL (Uniform Resource Locator)—Identifiers or addresses which find documents or sites on the Internet. URLs follow the form protocol://host/path/filename. Protocols guide searchers to the main (or default) directory of the servers. Exact files can be specified by including the path to the file. For example, to connect to The Citadel, use http://www.citadel.edu/citadel/otherserv/library

Virtual library—An organized collection of Internet sites where included sites have undergone a process of selection, description, and evaluation (such as *Magellan, Internet Public Library* and *Clearinghouse for Subject Oriented Resource Guides*). See Exercise 6 for information about specific virtual libraries.

Web browser—Also called Web clients, browsers retrieve and display information from Web servers and manage links between Web documents. Browsers can request information from almost any Internet server, including HTTP, Gopher, and FTP servers, and may be text-based (like Lynx) or graphical (like Netscape or Mosaic).

Step 1 Go to the following Web site:
http://www.nimh.nih.gov/

Step 2 Print a copy of the first page of the site.

Step 3. Identify components of the Web page by writing the letter corresponding to each component beside the appropriate place on the printout.

    A. URL
    B. Hypertext link
    C. Home page
    D. Toolbar
    E. Bookmark
    F. Back
    G. Forward
    H. Print
    I. Web browser

Step 4 If you are unable to print the page, answer the following questions about the Web site based on the screen display.
    A. What is the URL?
    B. What is the name of the home page?
    C. List one of the hypertext links.
    D. What is the Web browser?
    E. Where is the toolbar?
    F. List the "buttons" on the toolbar.

Internet Search Engines and Directories—Exercise 3

Some of the more popular Internet search engines and directories, and a description of how each works are listed below. The search engines contain help screens which provide detailed searching guidance, search tips, and examples. Reading help pages is well worth the effort and will ultimately save time.

Based on the descriptions below, choose two which would be useful for psychology research. With keywords identified for your research topic from Exercise 1, use those search engines to perform an Internet search. To access search engines, use either the URL provided, or the net search command of your Web browser.

Altavista—http://www.altavista.com
- Searches the Web as well as Usenet Newsgroups.
- Indexes entire Web page.
- Employs Boolean searching.
- Allows for simple and advanced queries.
- Advanced queries offer very sophisticated and specific search capability.

Example: depression and "academic achievement" or +depression+ "academic achievement"

Excite—http://www.excite.com
Searches the World Wide Web, Usenet, Usenet classifieds, and Excite's own database of Web site reviews.
- Indexes entire Web page.
- Has directory for browsing.

Example: +depression+academic "achievement" or depression and academic and achievement"

Infoseek http://infoseek.com
- Indexes Web pages, FTP sites, Gopher sites, Usenet Newsgroups, e-mail addresses.
- Indexes full text of Web pages.
- Very broad in scope.
- Search by keywords and phrases.
- Use very specific search queries.
- Has directory for browsing.

Example: "academic achievement" +depression

Lycos—http://www.lycos.com

- Very broad in scope.
- Searches full text of Web, Gopher sites, FTP sites, Usenet Newsgroups.
- Search results are based on a relevance ranking algorithm and assigned a score.
- Provides advanced searching capabilities.
- Creates abstracts of Web pages.
- Has directory for browsing.

Example: Type a phrase, such as <depression and grades> or <depression and college students>. Use the custom search feature.

MetaCrawler—http://metacrawler.com

Metacrawler relies on databases of various Web-based sources by sending queries to several web search engines and organizes results into a uniform format. It also provides an option of scoring hits, so that the displayed list can be sorted in several different ways, i.e.; locality, region, and organization.

Webcrawler—http://www.webcrawler.com

- Indexes Web pages, FTP sites and Gopher sites.
- WebCrawler provides keyword searching of titles and full texts of Web pages.
- Utilizes Boolean (i.e., AND, OR, NOT) operators.
- Boolean searching is recommended due to database size.
- Resulting hits are ranked.

*Example: depression **and** "academic achievement" **or** depression and academic **adj** achievement*

Yahoo—http://www.yahoo.com

- An Internet directory, using both human and machine intervention.
- A hierarchical, subject-oriented Web directory.
- Allows Boolean searching of titles, URLs, and comments fields—select "options."

Example: type < depression academic achievement>, click on options, then select desired option. Also try "academic achievement" +depression.

Keywords:_____

_____

_____

Search engine A:_____

Search engine B:_____

Answer the following questions based on results of each search.

1. Does the search engine provide advanced searching?

    Search engine A:

    Search engine B:

2. Does the "help" function provide searching tips?

    Search engine A:

    Search engine B:

3. If "yes" for questions 1. and/or 2., describe the recommendations given (for example, put phrases in quotation marks, or use Boolean operators).

    Search engine A:

    Search engine B:

4. How many results or "hits?"

    Search engine A:

    Search engine B:

5. Are results relevant to your research topic?

    Search engine A:

    Search engine B:

Evaluate Internet Sites—Exercise 4

Traditionally, research in psychology is presented in peer-reviewed journals which can be a long and demanding process. Internet sites provide new dimensions in transmitting information; information can be made known more quickly and be more widely distributed. However, results and conclusions may not be scrutinized as closely nor substantiated by empirically or scientifically-based research. Internet sites may also exist for reasons other than transmitting data and results, such as promoting a particular agenda by a site author or group.

For this exercise, choose one of the Internet sites listed in Appendix A. Access the site and evaluate it using the following questions as guides.

1. Name of Web site:

2. URL: http://

3. Who are the author(s) of this information?
   a. What are the author's reputation and credentials?
   b. What type of authority or experience do they have in this field?
   c. What is their affiliation?

4. What is the agenda of this site?
   a. Is this an advocacy group?
   b. Is this group or person objective?
   c. Is this an entertainment site?
   d. Is this a site for marketing products?

5. How current is this information?
   a. What is the posted date?
   b. Is this site maintained and updated?

6. How selective is the material?
   a. What is the breadth and depth of coverage?
   b. Is only material that supports one point of view included?

7. How accurate is the information?
   a. Are sources given for information?
   b. Can sources be verified?

Evaluate Internet Information—Exercise 5:

Using the same Web site as in Exercise 4, analyze information provided by the source.

1. Name of the Web site?_____

2. URL: http://
_____

3. LITERATURE REVIEW

a. Is this written for a professional or a layperson?

b. What are the theoretical assumptions?

c. Is treatment of the topic superficial or in-depth?

d. What is the hypothesis?

e. What is the independent variable?

f. What is the dependent variable?

4. METHOD

a. Is the method of the research provided?

b. Are the subjects described?

c. How are variables operationalized?

d. What are the experimental controls?

5. RESULTS

a. Are results provided?

b. Are methods of data analysis appropriate?

6. DISCUSSION

    a. Do results support the hypothesis?

    b. Is there discussion of ramifications and limitations of results?

    c. Do results support conclusions?

    d. Are results sensationalized or oversimplified?

    e. What other information should one have before one can agree or disagree with the conclusions?

    f. What are the ethical implications of this research?

7. REFERENCES

    a. Are references included?

    b. Are references appropriate for the topic?

    c. Are references current?

Virtual Libraries—Exercise 6

Virtual libraries are "value-added" Web sites which strive to organize and evaluate the Internet, much as a library does for its collection. They are created by applying traditional library science skills of identification, selection, organization, description, and evaluation of information to the Internet. Managers of virtual libraries continually search the Web for quality sites, including sites based on published criteria, and monitoring sites for quality.

Human intervention in development and maintenance of virtual libraries is both a strength and weakness. While the organization provides ease of use, and evaluative processes help assure quality, these attributes can also limit coverage. Virtual libraries are best used for research. Some Virtual libraries are:

The Argus Clearinghouse
http://www.clearinghouse.net/

Cyberhound
http://www.thomson.com/cyberhound/

Internet Public Library
http://ipl.org/

Magellan Internet Guide
http://www.mckinley.com/

Access one of the Internet libraries, peruse the information provided, and search for your topic, and answer the following questions.

1. What are criteria for inclusion in this Internet library?

2. Are criteria similar to evaluation criteria examined in Exercises 4 and 5?

3. How many hits resulted from the search?

4. How many hits are appropriate or relevant?

5. How do results from this search compare to results in Exercise 3 - using Internet search engines and directories?

Electronic Journals in Psychology—Exercise 7

Increasingly, journals are available via the Internet, however, it is a "mixed bag." Some journals allow free, full-text searching of all available issues, others allow searching of current issues only; some provide abstracts or tables of contents, others are only available by subscription.

This exercise gives students opportunities to know what journals are available electronically in their field, and experience a wide range of access capabilities.

1. Refer to **Electronic Journals (Appendix B)** for a list of journals and URLs.

2. Select two journals from this list.
   Journal A:_____

   Journal B:_____

3. Look for information on your research topic in each journal.

4. What type of information did each journal provide? Check Y for yes or N for no.

Journal A:

   full text_____   abstracts only_____   citations only_____   table of contents_____

   current issues and back files_____   current issue only___ back files only_____

   available only by subscription_____

Journal B:

   full text_____   abstracts only_____   citations only_____   table of contents_____

   current issues and back files_____   current issue only___ back files only_____

   available only by subscription_____

Citing Electronic Sources— Exercise 8

Information obtained from the Internet *must* be documented, just as one would document information from books and journal articles. All major style manuals provide guidance in correct citing of Internet sources. Additionally, this information is available online. Appendix C provides URLs and descriptions of Web sites containing citation information for The American Psychological Association (APA) style, the form preferred in psychology.

For this exercise, use information from these sites to put one of the previously identified Web sites into correct citation form.

Citation:

Appendix A: A Selective List of Psychology Web Sites

General Psychology Resources

American Psychoanalytic Association
http://apsa.org/

American Psychological Association PsychNET
http://www.apa.org

American Psychological Society
http://psych.hanover.edu/APS

Cognitive and Psychological Sciences on the Internet
http://matia.stanford.edu/cogsci.html

INFOMINE: Scholarly Internet Resource Collections
http://lib-www.ucr.edu/

PsychWeb
http://gasou.edu/psychweb/psychweb.htm

Yahoo's Psychology Page
http://www.yahoo.com/science/psychology/

Psychology History

The Freud Web
http://twine.stg.brown.edu/projects/hypertext/landow/HTatBrown/freud/Freud_OV.html

Clinical and Counseling Psychology

National Institute of Mental Health
http://www.nimh.nih.gov/

Mental Health Resources
http://www.cityscape.co.uk/users/ad88/resuk.htm

PsychStar Homepage - University of Michigan
http://www.psych.med.umich.edu/

The GROHOL Mental Health Page
http://www.coil.com/~grohol/

FreudNet: The A.A. Brill Library
http://plaza.interport.net/nypsan/

A Page of Dreams
http://lucien.berkeley.edu/dreams.html

Dreamlink
http://www.iag.net/~hutchib/.dream/

Depression Central
http://www.psycom.net/depression.central.html

Educational Psychology

UC Berkeley School of Psychology
http://www-gse.berkeley.edu/program/SP/sp.html

ERIC Clearinghouse
http://www.ericsp.org/

Teaching Educational Psychology SIG—American Educational Research Association
http://seamonkey.ed.asu.edu/~gene/TEPSIG/TEP_SIG.html

Developmental Psychology

Center for Adolescent Studies - University of Indiana
http://education.indiana.edu/cas/cashmpg.html

Mental Health Risk Factors for Adolescents - University of Indiana
http://education.indiana.edu/cas/adol/mental.html

Ritual Abuse, Ritual Crime, and Healing Home Page
http://www.xroads.com/rahome

The Arc - Mental retardation issues
http://fohnix.metronet.com/~thearc/welcome.html

Centre for Neuro Skills Home Page
http://www.callamer.com/~cns/

Appendix B: Electronic Journals in Psychology

Education Theory
http://www.ed.uiuc.edu/coe/eps/Educational-Theory/ET-welcome.html

Mental Health OT
http://www.iop.bpmf.ac.uk/home/trust/ot/aotmhmag.htm

JAMA, The Journal of the American Medical Association
http://www.ama-assn.org/public/journals/jama/jamahome.htm

Journal of Cognitive Neuroscience
http://www-mitpress.mit.edu:80/jrnls-catalog/cognitive-abstracts/cog.html

Lancet
http://www.thelancet.com/

Latin American Journal of Psychology
http://www.psy.utexas.edu/psy/RLP/RLP-welcome.html

Neuroscience-Net
http://www.neuroscience.com/buttons.html

New England Journal of Medicine
http://www.nejm.org/

Psychological Assessment
http://www.apa.org/journals/pas.html

Psychological Methods
http://www.apa.org/journals/met.html

Psychological Review
http://www.apa.org/journals/rev.html

The Self-Help Psychology Magazine
http://www.well.com/user/selfhelp/

Appendix C Citing Electronic Sources

APA Publication Manual Crib Sheet by Russ Dewey
http://www.gasou.edu/psychweb/tipsheet/apacrib.htm#discussion
This document includes discussion on proper formatting of bibliographic entries for ftp, gopher, and web documents, and gives examples of each.

Web Extension to American Psychological Association Style (WEAPAS) by T. Land.
http://www.beadsland.com/weapas/
As the title implies, the guide elaborates on the APA style. It assumes some familiarity with APA style, and does not include any examples. Instead, it attempts to describe various forms that citation elements may take in an electronic document.

Guide for Citing Electronic Information by K. Wagner
http://www.wilpaterson.edu/wpcpages/library/citing.htm.
This guide is based on the 1993 style manual by Li and Crane (see below), and includes examples from most forms of electronic documents.

Bibliographic Formats for Citing Electronic Information by Xia Li and Nancy Crane.
http://www.uvm.edu/~ncrane/estyles
This guide includes information on following both the APA and the MLA citation styles.

Notes: